From Day
to Dinner

A GOURMET'S GUIDE TO
MUSHROOM COOKERY
WITH SELECTED RECIPES
FROM MASTER CHEFS

EDITED BY MARJORIE YOUNG AND VINCE VIVERITO

Seasonal Feasts

From Duff to Dinner: A Gourmet's Guide to Mushroom Cookery

Edited by Marjorie R. Young and Vince Viverito

Cover art by Gay Kraeger

Copyright 1998 by Marjorie R. Young and Vince Viverito

ISBN 1-890880-02-7

Manufactured in the United States

Published by: Seasonal Feasts
PO Box 1463
Los Gatos, CA 95031
fax: 408 353-8767

An imprint of Aqua Thermal Access
55 Azalea Lane, Santa Cruz, CA 95060
phone and fax: 408 426-2956
e-mail: hsprings@ix.netcom.com

Acknowledgments

This book would have been impossible to produce without the assistance of many friends and colleagues. Members of the Santa Cruz Fungus Federation contributed recipes and suggestions. Their names have been noted with their favorite recipes.

The recipes, printed with permission, from the various chefs and restaurants we contacted were provided with enthusiasm and encouragement.

Thank you to Gay Kraeger who designed our cover and provided all of the wonderful drawings. Gay and Felicity Christensen share the honors in coming up with the title for the book.

Chef Joseph Cirone who, in addition to contributing many fine recipes, was always available to answer any questions we had and provided us with the introduction and back cover copy.

The Mushroom Gods will surely smile down on Chef Jozseph Schultz who went out of his way to provide us with recipes and commentary in his own inimitable fashion. Kudos.

Our gratitutde to Arleen Bessette whose salient observations and attention to detail helped to make this book a cohesive work, and to Debra Johnson whose keen eye helped to improve the accuracy of both the recipes and general content.

A special thank you to our spouses who were always available to assist us as we encountered the many problems which always seem to occur while trying to put together a book.

> To Susanne. my lovely wife, for proofreading and editing every page, and offering suggestions that made the copy comprehensible. Your support was much appreciated.
>
> Vince Viverito

> To Henry, who patiently dealt with one computer crisis after another. His knowledge of mushrooms, both scientific and culinary, was extremely valuable.
>
> Marjorie Young

From the Editors

This book is about cooking with mushrooms, both domestic and wild. Many of these recipes are quite unusual and hopefully will provide you with some gourmet experiences. Whenever you are using mushrooms for consumption, be certain of their edibility. Each person's reaction to the edibility of a specific mushroom is very different. If you have never tried one of the recommended species suggested in a recipe, it is a good idea to cook up a small bit first, try it, and wait twenty-four hours to make sure you do not experience any gastric upset.

This book is not about identifying mushrooms. We recommend that you join a mycological society if you want to scramble around in the duff (the decaying matter on the forest floor where many of the mushrooms are found) and pick your own. The expert advice and identification assistance you will receive will prove invaluable. Remember, "When in doubt, throw it out." Never eat a mushroom if you have any question as to its identity.

The small chef's hat perched above the title of a recipe indicates that the recipe was provided by one of the wonderful, generous, master chefs who gave us, with the ingredients, detailed instructions and helpful comments. Read their biographies in the introductory section and, as a special treat when you are in the area, visit their restaurants and further enjoy their culinary skills.

We decided to do this book because both of our families enjoy cooking and eating from recipes which sometimes use slightly unusual ingredients but still maintain the integrity of the mushroom taste. The alternative mushroom suggestions made in many of the recipes are our ideas. Please, try out your own, using your favorite mushrooms which may differ based on time of year and physical location as well as your tastebuds. We have enjoyed putting this book together. We hope you will experience many pleasurable dining experiences using it.

Marjorie Young and Vince Viverito

Contents

Introduction   10

Chefs' Biographies   12

Recipes

Appetizers   15

Smoked Shiitakes   17
Crab Stuffed Morels   18
Wild Mushroom Phyllo   19
Chanterelle Rice Paper Rolls   20
Budino Di Porcini e Tartufi   22
Craterellus Spread   24
Portobello Mushrooms Mediterranean Style   25
Funghi Griglia con Polenta e Marscarpone   26
Mushroom Strudel   28
Russian Blini   30
Chanterelle Caviar in Puff Pastry   31
Craterellus Paté   32
Chanterelle Bacon   34
Matsutake Fondue   35
Gregg Ferguson's Stuffed Morels   36

Soups and Salads   37

Soups

Cream of Morel Soup   39
Winter Mushroom and Chestnut Bisque   40
Golden Matsutake   42
Wild Mushroom Soup   43
Mushroom-Coconut Milk Soup/Curry   44
Bisque of Chanterelles   46
Boletus Barley Soup   47
Rumanian Tart Soup with Boletes   48

7

Salads

Warm Endive Salad with Chanterelles,
    Enoki and Asparagus   50
Boletos Caroenum, Hot or Cold Tree Fungus Salad   51
Mushroom Tortellini Salad   52
Lalap Djamur   54
Grilled Corn, Asparagus, and Mushroom Salad   56

The Main Course   57

Fresh Swordfish Steak "a la Japonais"
    with Mushrooms   59
Braised Trout with Mushroom Sauce   60
Mushroom Stuffed Enchiladas   62
Crayfish Fettuccine   63
French-Canadian Meat and Mushroom Tart   64
Holiday Goose with Mushroom Stuffing
    and Grape Sauce   66
Oak Forest Pie   68
Eggs Benedict with Morels   69
Bacon 'N Bolete Quiche   70
Grilled Thai Seabass with Portobello Compote   72
Puffballs with Scallops and Broccoli   73
Glazed Chicken with Chanterelle-Sunflower
    Stuffing   74
Wild Mushroom Flan   76
Any Mushroom Pie   77
Sautéed Shiitake with Scallops   78
Chicken Baked with Chanterelles and Cream   79
Lasagna of Woodland Mushrooms over
    Balsamic Lentils   80
Squash-Mushroom Pie   83
Wild Mushroom Lasagna   84
Variations on a Theme—Basic Sauces with Mushrooms   86

Side Dishes 87

    Vegetables with Porcini Dressing 89
    Fettuccine with Shiitake Mushrooms
       and Fresh Tomato Sauce 90
    Yorkshire Pudding, San Francisco Dos Rios 92
    Tagliatelle con Funghi 93
    Mushroom Custards 94
    Scalloped Potatoes with Sparassis 96

Baked Goods and Desserts 97

  Baked Goods

    Candy Cap and Pecan Scones 99
    Pine Spike and Potato Bread 100
    Blewit Batter Bread 102

  Desserts

    Candy Cap Cheesecake 104
    Candy Cap Cornmeal Loaf 106
    Almond Candy Cap Cookies 107
    Dessert Toppings 108

Index to Mushrooms Used in Recipes 110

Recipe Index 113

Introduction
Joseph M. Cirone, Executive Chef
Goosetown Caffe

To eat and to appreciate the flavor of mushrooms is to transcend the ordinary and eliminate the mundane in everyday dishes. Their uses in the culinary arts of every culture both past and present, as well as the reputed healing value of some species, are well known. Mushrooms are inherently global.

From the fryer to the oven and from mere appetizers to desserts, it is difficult to find an equal to the mushroom. Both the "wild," some of which are now commonly cultivated and available at a price, and the domestic, are extensively pervasive in any reputable menu. The public demands it, and the subtleties of each variety and their properties will transform an ordinary dish to the extraordinary.

In our experience, we see mushrooms treated in five ways: fresh, dried, pickled, frozen or canned. Although we choose only to use fresh fungi, it is beneficial to understand the difficulties and subtleties that lie in the use of mushrooms in each of these states.

Warm water or room temperature wines should be used when rehydrating dehydrated mushrooms, and the liquid should be reserved, not discarded after completion, to be used either in the recipe being prepared or as a base for sauce or soups. Dried mushrooms should generally be held in the freezer to prevent decay. Pickling tends to obliterate the unique flavor of each species, but still may be useful for serving a specific need. This brings to mind a general rule that we try to obey in our kitchen when we are handling mushrooms. We use acids, such as citric acids, wines or vinegar, with extreme caution when combining with mushrooms. They have a tendency to mask the flavor of the mushrooms.

Technology has also made strides toward freezing and packing frozen mushrooms. Exotics that were once unavailable in many areas, or foraged only seasonally, now may be readily available in many areas. Although the flavor and quality of these may be debated and largely inconsistent, they may prove useful in a pinch. Canned mushrooms should be used only as a last resort.

When handling fresh mushrooms, it is best to use the following guideline: plan ahead. If the mushrooms are going to be used fresh, then they should be used within four or five days of refrigeration. Mushrooms should be stored in cloth sacks or wax or paper bags when refrigerated, NEVER in plastic bags. Be sure to clean mushrooms just before use and not before storage, due to the fact that excessive moisture may expedite the decaying of fresh mushrooms while in refrigeration.

Different mushrooms should be cleaned in different ways. Trimming the base of the stem to remove soil should be completed before cleaning, preferably in the field if you are gathering wild mushrooms. Tools that are indispensable in cleaning are the paring knife, a mushroom brush, a clean toothbrush, and a damp rag. Delicate fungi such as hedgehogs should be rinsed in warm water before being brushed gently and scraped with a paring knife. Durable portobellos may be scrubbed with a damp cloth and rinsed under running water. Boletes and similar types should be scrubbed with a damp cloth and liberal use of the toothbrush. Cleaning with water should be avoided when grilling or sautéing mushrooms since the additional moisture may cause them to become mushy during cooking. Chanterelles should be dry sautéed over high heat whenever possible.

In general, we emphasize simplicity when using mushrooms. Let the flavor and subtlety of each species pervade the dish while not being masked by over seasoning for an aggressive palate....simple flavors...exotic combinations. These are easier to achieve every year with the advances in cultivation as well as foraging.

From the simple Champignons des Paris to the exotic morel, we continue to challenge ourselves to exploit the nuances found in each of the species to please the insatiable palate and to satisfy our own creativity.

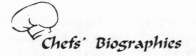

Chefs' Biographies

Chef Carolyn Allen is head chef at Paolo's, located at 333 W. San Carlos, San Jose, 408 294-2558. She grew up in the business and is the daughter of Jack Allen, Paolo's retired owner. Paolo's is one of the finest Italian restaurants in the Bay Area.

Executive Chef *Tony Baker* makes an outstanding vegetarian (if you don't mind eggs, milk or cheese among other things) lasagna dish that is really unique. You can find Tony at Montrio, an American Bistro located at 414 Calle Principal, Monterey, 408 648-8880.

Executive Chef Joseph M. Cirone can be found at Goosetown Caffe in the Willow Glen district of San Jose. Located at 1075 Lincoln Avenue, 408 292-4866, Goosetown offers the distinctive cuisine of southern Italy.

Michelle Dey is chef at the Stockton Bridge Grille, 231 Esplanade, Capitola-by-the-Sea, (Santa Cruz area), 408-462-1350. Stockton Bridge Grille is nestled at the mouth of the Soquel River with a panoramic view of the Monterey Bay. The menu specializes in imaginative seafood and assorted pasta dishes with an extensive California wine list. Michelle is an honors graduate of the California Culinary Academy in San Francisco and worked in the dining room of the Ritz Carlton before coming to the beautiful Santa Cruz area.

Executive chef *Clyde G. Griesbach III* is currently at Brandon's in the Beverly Heritatge Hotel, 1820 Barber Lane, San Jose, 408 943-9087. He was named chef of the year for the South Bay in 1990 by Chefs of America. While treating diners with his creations at Paolo's, the restaurant was voted the best Italian restaurant in Northern California by the Zagat Guide in 1994.

Emile Mooser is the owner and Executive Chef of Emile's Restaurant located at 545 South Second Street, San Jose, 408 289-1960. Emile's has been famous in San Jose for its contemporary European cuisine since 1973 and was declared the best traditional French restaurant in the San Francisco Bay Area by Zagat. Other awards for Emile's include the Wine Spectator "Award of Excellence," the "Travel Holiday Award" since 1979, and the "DiRoNA Award" since 1985 (Distinguished Restaurant of America Award). Emile is the winner of ten Gold Medals and 2 Grand Prix Awards in culinary competition.

The Fishwife restaurant at Asilomar Beach in Pacific Grove is owned by *Julio J. Ramirez*, C.E.C. and *Maria Perucca-Ramirez*, and has been voted the best seafood restaurant in Monterey County for the last eight years in a row by readers of "Coast Weekly." It is located at 19961/2 Sunset Drive, Pacific Grove, 408-375-7107.

Julio and Maria also own the Turtle Bay Taqueria located at 1301 Fremont Boulevard, Seaside, 408 899-1010. Turtle Bay's menu was inspired by trips to the Caribbean, Yucatan, and Belize and offers a selection of these cuisines. The recipe "Fettuccine with Shiitake Mushrooms and Fresh Tomato Sauce" comes to us from their book *The Crocodile's Cookbook, Bounty of the Americas,* and is reprinted with their permission.

Jozseph Schultz was the founder, owner and chef of India Joze, a very popular restaurant in Santa Cruz that continues to use his unusual recipes and ideas. He is also an author and has kindly allowed us to reprint several of his recipes from his book *The Mushroom Cookbook*, 1996. As a "raconteur par excellence," his cooking demonstrations are a treat for all of the senses. He can be reached by e-mail at mwatch@cruzio.com.

Jozseph's unique philosophy is expressed in this excerpt adapted from his book. *"Mushrooms are wonderful in textures and aromas, but they are often low in intensity of flavor. All foods taste best when there is at least a little of all flavors present. Familiar and unfamiliar recipes can benefit from the addition of the six flavors...sweet, sour, hot/pungent, bitter, salty, and rich, especially the ones that seem to be missing. The forms these flavors take can be exotic and expensive or everyday items. Try a little pimento or sugar for sweet, a little tamarind or lemon juice for sour, a little scotch or chili for hot/pungent, a little bitter melon or black pepper for bitter, a little fish sauce or salt for salty, or a little roasted sesame oil or olive oil for richness. The inquisitive spirit of the seasoned mushroom hunter belongs in the kitchen as much as the field."*

THE
RECIPES

APPETIZERS

Smoked Shiitakes   17
Crab Stuffed Morels   18
Wild Mushroom Phyllo   19
Chanterelle Rice Paper Rolls   20
Budino Di Porcini e Tartufi   22
Craterellus Spread   24
Portobello Mushrooms Mediterranean Style   25
Funghi Griglia con Polenta e Marscarpone   26
Mushroom Strudel   28
Russian Blini   30
Chanterelle Caviar in Puff Pastry   31
Craterellus Paté   32
Chanterelle Bacon   34
Matsutake Fondue   35
Gregg Ferguson's Stuffed Morels   36

Smoked Shiitakes

Contributed by Chef Jozseph Schultz

This adaptation of a Balinese technique makes wonderful hor d'oeuvres. The shiitake (*Lentinus edodes*) stems are a little tough, but they make great handles to pick up the mushroom. Line your wok with aluminum foil or use an old wok you don't want to use for anything else.

½ *pound whole smallish fresh shiitakes*
1 *teaspoon peanut oil (optional)*
2 *tablespoons balsamic vinegar*
1 *tablespoon soy sauce*
1 *teaspoon sugar (optional)*
·1 *tablespoon fresh mashed garlic paste*
¼ *teaspoon ground black pepper*

1 *cup rice hulls, or substitute rice.*
  Soak briefly if you have time.
¼ *cup sugar*
¼ *cup tea leaves (optional)*

Mix oil, vinegar, soy sauce, sugar, garlic and pepper. Toss with mushrooms.

Line wok with aluminum foil. Put rice, sugar and tea in wok. Heat over medium heat until smoking.

Reduce heat. Place mushrooms on rack over smoke. Cover and smoke ½ hour to 1 hour.

Serve warm or cold, with a spicy relish.

Serves 4

Crab Stuffed Morels

Contributed by Phil Carpenter

You might try substituting any mushroom with a cap suitable for stuffing for the morel (*Morchella sp.*).

In the field these can be cooked by steaming in a covered skillet using a little water or white wine for moisture.

Stuffing mixture

8 ounces of soft cream cheese
2 tablespoons finely chopped shallots
½ teaspoon finely chopped garlic
2 tablespoons soy sauce
6-8 ounces chopped crab meat (imitation seems to work fine and is less costly.)
1-2 tablespoons finely chopped Italian parsley (optional)
pepper to taste

12-18 medium to large fresh morels (Morchella sp.) or substitute

Preheat oven to 350 degrees F.

Combine the stuffing mixture ingredients in a medium to large bowl. Carefully slice each morel lengthwise along one side only (do not cut through both sides). If using cap type mushrooms fill each cap with the stuffing mix.

Partially open the morels, being careful not to tear the mushrooms in half, and fill with the stuffing mixture until the cavity is completely full to slightly heaping. Place on a dry or very lightly greased cookie sheet (Pam works well here) and bake in a preheated oven at 350 degrees F. for approximately 10 to 15 minutes or until the mushrooms are soft.

Serves 4 to 8 depending on size of morels

Wild Mushroom Phyllo

If using fresh mushrooms, mince very fine, including the stems. If dry are used, rehydrate in warm water for 20 minutes then drain and pat dry on a paper towel, then mince fine. *Boletus edulis* would be particularly good.

1 pound fresh or 4 ounces dried of your favorite "meaty" mushroom, minced fine
3 tablespoons butter
1 tablespoon oil
2 large leeks, whites only, finely chopped
1/4 cup fresh finely chopped chives
1/2 cup sour cream
1 teaspoon dried dill weed (or to taste)
1/2 teaspoon salt, or to taste
1/4 teaspoon fresh ground pepper, or to taste
Package of phyllo dough refrigerated until ready to use

Remove phyllo from fridge and allow to come to room temperature.

Preheat oven to 350 degrees.

Melt the butter and heat the oil in a 10-12 inch skillet over moderate heat. Sauté mushrooms, leeks and chives until all the moisture has evaporated, about 10 minutes. Set aside to cool.

Add the sour cream, dill, salt and pepper, stirring to blend thoroughly.

Melt 1/2 cup butter in a small saucepan over low heat and set aside. Cut the phyllo into 8 strips 2x18 inches and wrap in a moist towel. Take one of the strips from the towel and place 1 teaspoon of filling at the bottom end of the strip and fold the corner over to form a triangle. Continue folding like a flag. Cover each triangle with a moist towel until ready to bake.

Brush each triangle with the reserved butter on all sides, and place on a cookie sheet and bake for 20 minutes. Serve at once.

Serves about 30 as an appetizer

Chanterelle Rice Paper Rolls

Contributed by Debra Johnson

Dipping sauce: Trader Joe's Peanut Sauce is good, but it needs to be thinned slightly. An alternative would be a broth, soy, vinegar, fish sauce, green onion, and chile mix to taste.

rice wrappers (round, crisp, found in Asian markets)
3/4 pound fresh mung bean sprouts
basil leaves, fresh, one bunch
mint leaves, fresh, one bunch
green onions, one bunch sliced
Thin rice noodles (can substitute bean thread noodles)
1/2 pound cooked shrimp (cut shrimp in two mirror-image halves to reduce bulk)
3/4 pound fresh chanterelles (Cantharellus cibarius), sliced

Microwave chanterelles covered with juice of one lemon until the juices are released, 5 or 6 minutes. Be sure not to overcook them as you want them to taste fresh.

Wash and drain bean sprouts. Wash basil and mint, trimming and separating into whole leaves.

Pour boiling water over bean thread noodles in a bowl; let sit to soften. They're ready when they're slippery-tender, maybe 10 minutes.

Set a baking dish or large pie pan in the sink. Fill the pan with boiling or very hot water. You'll use this to soften the rice wrappers. Place a wrapper in the water and you'll see it soften. Lift carefully out of the water and lay flat. (Be sure you wear your asbestos fingers, not your regular ones!)

I like to use a sushi rolling mat, as the wrapper doesn't seem to stick as readily as to a plate or cutting board. Lay ingredients crosswise on the wrapper, on the third closest to you: A couple of shrimp, a few leaves each of mint and basil, a few green onion bits, 1 or 2 pieces of chanterelle, a small bunch of noodles you've fished out of the soaking water and drained. You can add a smear of peanut sauce if desired. Wrap together like a burrito, folding sides in as you go and rolling away from you.

Place on waxed paper and refrigerate until serving. They really should be eaten within a few hours but will keep a bit longer if you place a damp towel, then plastic wrap, over all.

Makes 12-18 servings

Budino Di Porcini e Tartufi

Contributed by Chef Carolyn Allen

2 tablespoons butter
1/4 cup onion, finely diced
1/4 cup dried porcini
   (Boletus edulis) mushrooms
   soaked in warm water to cover for
   30 minutes
1/4 cup beef stock (canned stock is okay,
   but home made is better)
1 tablespoon white truffle butter (can be
   purchased at specialty food stores)

3 egg yolks
1 cup milk
salt and white pepper to taste
dash nutmeg

1 russet potato (large)
2 tablespoons melted butter
white truffle oil (can be purchased at
   specialty food stores)
2 tablespoons finely chopped chives

Sauté onions with butter over low heat till translucent. Turn heat up to medium and cook until dark golden and caramelized.

Strain porcini soaking liquid through cheesecloth and add it to the onions. Add porcini mushrooms and beef stock and let simmer on medium heat till the liquid has turned syrupy and almost evaporated. Remove from heat and stir in the truffle butter. Let cool.

Put porcini mixture, egg yolks and milk in a food processor or blender and puree. Strain through a sieve, pushing the liquid and solids through as much as possible. Taste for salt and pepper and add the dash of nutmeg.

Butter 6 4-ounce custard molds. Pour in the porcini mixture. Place the custard molds in a large pan water bath about 1/2 way up the sides of the molds. Cover the pan with foil and place in a 325 degree F. preheated oven for 25 minutes or until a sharp knife inserted in center comes out clean.

Peel potato and with a mandoline or cheese slicer cut into 18 paper thin slices lengthwise.

Soak slices in cold water for 15 minutes. Drain and thoroughly dry potato slices. Brush with melted butter on both sides and place on a nonstick cookie sheet or one lined with parchment paper. Set oven at 275 degrees and bake potato slices for approximately 15 minutes, turning once, or until light golden brown and crisp.

Run the end of a sharp, thin-bladed knife around the edge of each custard mold. Unmold each Budino and surround with 3 potato crisps. Drizzle a bit of white truffle oil over each Budino and sprinkle with chives.

Serves 6

Craterellus Spread

Craterellus cornucopioides is commonly know as craterellus or horn of plenty.

*1 cup fresh craterellus, chopped fine, or,
1/2 cup dried and crumbled,
reconstituted in just enough water to
cover, then drained thoroughly*

*8 ounce container of whipped cream
cheese
1/3 cup sour cream
1 large clove garlic, mashed
1 heaping tablespoon finely chopped onion*

2 tablespoons butter
salt

Sauté the craterellus in the butter until thoroughly cooked; add a dash of salt.

Mix the rest of the ingredients in a bowl until well blended. Add the mushrooms.

Refrigerate overnight or for several hours to give flavors a chance to blend.

Spread on crackers or toast rounds.

Makes 2 cups

Portobello Mushrooms Mediterranean Style

These meaty tasting mushrooms can now be used as a basis for a sandwich, sliced over pasta, on top of a pizza or over steaks or chicken. They can, of course be served warm as the entrée of a vegetarian meal. Two per person would be ideal for a main course. You can also use them as the main ingredient in Pitas and wraps. Portobellos are a variety of *Agaricus bisporus*.

6 portobello mushrooms four to six inches in diameter (don't wash in water)
10 cloves fresh garlic, peeled
2 tablespoons extra virgin olive oil
1 teaspoon fresh lemon juice
2 teaspoons balsamic vinegar
salt and pepper to taste

Preheat oven to 400 degrees F.

Press the garlic cloves into a small bowl. Add the olive oil, lemon juice, balsamic vinegar, salt and pepper and mix well. Place the mushrooms gill side up in a baking pan. Spread the garlic mixture equally over the mushrooms being carefully not to break the delicate gills. Lightly salt each mushroom.

Bake in the preheated oven for 15 to 20 minutes, (mushrooms are done when liquid begins leaking from the cap). Remove from oven and cool.

Serves 6 to 8 as an appetizer (3 as an entrée)

Funghi Griglia con Polenta e Marscarpone

Contributed by Chef Carol Allen

Marscarpone is a rich, faintly tart Italian cream cheese. You can find it in cheese stores, specialty food stores, or Italian markets. An absolutely superb appetizer that would go well with a glass of fine Chianti or a Cabernet.

12 large shiitake (Lentinus edodes) or
   4 portobello mushrooms (a variety of
   Agaricus bisporus) stems removed
5 sprigs fresh rosemary, 1 coarsely
   minced, 4 left whole for garnish
1 sprig fresh sage, coarsely minced
1 sprig fresh thyme, coarsely minced
2 lemons
salt and pepper to taste
the best extra-virgin olive oil you can find
1 cup polenta
1 cup water or chicken stock (preferred)
1 cup milk
1/4 teaspoon salt
2 tablespoons butter
1/4 cup grated Parmesan cheese
   (optional)
4 tablespoons Marscarpone

Prepare the polenta by combining water, milk and salt in a saucepan and bringing to a boil. Gradually add the polenta in a thin stream stirring constantly. Turn down the heat, letting the polenta cook at a low simmer. Continue stirring for about 15 minutes. Stir in butter (and cheese if desired), cover, remove from heat and keep warm until ready to serve.

Cut one lemon in slices about 1/4 inch thick (you need 4 slices). Brush mushroom caps on both sides with the olive oil. Place caps top–side down on a medium–hot grill. Cut one lemon in half and squeeze juice over the grilling caps. Brush lemon slices with olive oil and place on the grill. Sprinkle mushrooms with salt and pepper and the minced herbs.

Let the caps grill for about 3 or 4 minutes or until they "relax" or droop a little, then turn them over and sprinkle with a bit more lemon juice, herbs, salt and pepper. Turn lemon slices over and continue grilling. Grill mushrooms and lemon slices for another 2 to 3 minutes or until mushrooms are slightly limp. NOTE: If you don't have a grill you can do this step in a medium hot wok.

Put a large spoon of soft, steamy polenta in the center of each plate. Put a tablespoon of Marscarpone in the center of the polenta. Overlap three mushrooms atop the polenta and Marscarpone, anoint with a drizzle of olive oil.

Garnish the plates with the lemon slices and whole rosemary sprigs. Serve.

Serves 4

Mushroom Strudel

8 ounces fresh shiitake (Lentinus edodes),
   oyster (Pleurotus ostreatus), or almost
   any wild mushroom
8 ounces store mushrooms
   (Agaricus bisporus)
6 green onions, sliced
3 tablespoons margarine or butter
3 tablespoons white wine
2 tablespoons diced pimiento
2 tablespoons chopped parsley
1/4 teaspoon pepper
1/8 teaspoon dried thyme, crushed
1 egg yolk
6 sheets phyllo dough (18x12-inch
   rectangles)
1/4 cup margarine or butter
2 tablespoons fine bread crumbs

Preheat oven to 400 degrees F.

After removing any woody stems, coarsely chop mushrooms.

In a heavy skillet cook mushrooms and onions in the 3 tablespoons butter for 4 to 5 minutes or until tender. Add wine and cook on high for 2 to 3 minutes or until liquid has evaporated. Remove from heat and stir in pimiento, parsley, pepper, and thyme. Cool 10 minutes.

Place half the mixture in a food processor and add the egg yolk. Cover and process until fine. Recombine with remaining mixture.

Cut the sheets of phyllo dough in half crosswise. (You should end up with twelve 12 x 9 sheets.) Cover the sheets with a damp towel and be sure to keep the dough covered as you work.

Layer six half-sheets of the phyllo on a large ungreased baking sheet, brushing butter between each sheet. Sprinkle half the bread crumbs toward one side of the sheets leaving 3 inches from the long edge and 1 1/2 inches from the ends.

Spoon half of the mushroom mixture over the bread crumbs. Fold in the short ends and roll up starting with the side nearest the filling. Brush roll with melted butter. Cut diagonal slits through the top layer of dough only, down the roll about 1 inch apart.

Repeat process to make second roll.

Bake in 400 degree F. oven for 15 to 18 minutes or until golden. Cool 5 minutes.

Using a serrated knife, cut the rolls completely through at the diagonal slits.

Serves 12 to 16

Russian Blini

Contributed by Henry Young

The blini can be served on a silver tray with champagne or they can be made while camping if you use a prepared pancake mix. Almost any mushroom will work but one with a firm texture would be best, such as *Boletus edulis.*

2 cups buckwheat flour
1 cup all-purpose flour
1 teaspoon sugar
2 teaspoons salt
1 package active dry yeast
1 cup warm water (105-115 degrees F.)
2 cups warm milk
1/4 cup melted butter
butter to fry blini and mushrooms
48 thinly sliced large pieces of mushroom
    if using smaller mushrooms, more slices
    are needed
small container sour cream
small jar of caviar

Combine buckwheat flour, all-purpose flour, sugar, and salt.

Sprinkle yeast onto warm water and let stand for a few minutes, then stir to dissolve.

Add milk and butter. Stir into the dry mixture and beat until smooth. Put in a warm place to rise for several hours.

Add a bit of water to batter if necessary as blini should be thin. Melt about 2 tablespoons of butter in a heavy skillet and add enough batter to make a blini about 3 inches around. Cook until brown on both sides. Put on platter and assemble.

While batter is rising, sauté the mushrooms until almost crispy in butter and oil.

To assemble: Smear small amount of sour cream on blini, top with one or two pieces of mushroom. Add a dollop more of the sour cream and a bit of caviar and serve.

Makes 4 dozen blini

Chanterelle Caviar in Puff Pastry

Contributed by Susanne Viverito

6 tablespoons butter
1/2 pound fresh chanterelles, finely
    chopped
4 medium shallots, minced
1 tablespoon sweet vermouth or white wine
1 garlic clove, minced
2 tablespoons toasted pine nuts,
    crushed
1 to 2 tablespoons sour cream
1 puff pastry sheet

Preheat oven to 350 degrees F (or follow baking directions on pastry sheet package).

Melt 3 tablespoons of the butter in a 8-10 inch frying pan over moderate heat and sauté the chanterelles, shallots, garlic and pine nuts until all moisture is gone (about 10 minutes).

Add the sour cream and vermouth or wine, blend well and set aside.

Melt the remaining 3 tablespoons of butter over low heat and set aside.

Cut the pastry sheet into 20 squares and place some of the mushroom mixture into the center of each square. Gather the 4 corner points together and brush to cover with the 3 tablespoons of butter.

Place the filled pastries on a cookie sheet and bake for about 20 minutes or until lightly browned.

Serve at once.

Makes 20

Craterellus Paté

Contributed by Felicity Christensen

"This paté has one very endearing feature. You can alter the ingredients as much as you like and it still turns out great. Choose any strongly flavored mushroom. I prefer using dried craterellus as the flavor is more intense after it has dried."

Felicity

3 to 4 ounces dried craterellus (Craterellus cornucopioides) reconstituted in brandy or 6 ounces of other fresh mushroom brandy if needed to reconstitute mushrooms

4 tablespoons butter
1/2 cup finely chopped shallots
2 (or more) chopped garlic cloves
12 ounces button mushrooms (Agaricus bisporus)–cremini have more flavor
salt and pepper to taste
2 to 3 tablespoons fruity brandy if using all fresh mushrooms and there is no liquid left from reconstituting the dried ones (pear, apple, or plain brandy mixed with triple sec or cointreau works well)
2 tablespoons chopped fresh tarragon (parsley or thyme will do in a pinch)
3 to 4 tablespoons heavy cream
1 cup walnuts, pecans or hazelnuts
juice of 1 lemon

Cover the mushrooms in brandy and leave for about 45 minutes. Drain mushrooms, squeezing the excess brandy out. Reserve the liquid for later use.

Roughly chop all of the mushrooms.

Melt the butter in a large skillet over medium heat. Sauté shallots and garlic until soft, approximately 5 minutes.

Add the mushrooms, salt and pepper. Turn up the heat and cook, stirring constantly until the mushrooms give up their liquid. Add the brandy and herbs and cook until all the liquid evaporates.

This paté freezes well. Make sure to get as much air out before freezing it by covering it first with plastic wrap and then with foil. It is best served at room temperature.

Pour in the cream and stir. Boil until the cream evaporates and the pan is almost dry.

Transfer to a blender. Add the nuts and process until you have a fine, spreadable texture, but the nuts are still chunky.

Season to taste with salt, pepper and lemon juice. Mix well and set aside to cool to room temperature.

Serve in a crock with crackers or a good baguette.

Makes 2 cups

Chanterelle Bacon

Contributed by Chef Jozseph Schultz

Serving suggestions: mound the chanterelles in small, boiled potatoes which have been partially scooped out and lightly seasoned with salt and pepper; sprinkle on your favorite salad; or use as the topping on a cracker stacked with a cucumber slice, and sour cream or cream cheese.

Chanterelles (Cantharellus cibarius), well cleaned, sliced thin.

Oil, preferably a neutral vegetable oil like peanut oil. Bacon fat is also excellent and will impart a hint of bacon flavor to the mushrooms.

Heat oil in a skillet or wok over high heat. Add chanterelles and stir until pieces stop sizzling.

Depending upon the amount of mushrooms and the heat of your stove, this could take 3 to 15 minutes or more. Once most of the water is boiled out, the chanterelles need to be closely monitored to prevent burning. They will seem a little limp even when they are done. If they are insufficiently toasted they will be tough.

Drain on paper towels.

Seal well to store.

Serves 4

Matsutake Fondue

Fun for Two

You will need metal or wooden bamboo skewers and a fondue pot or the like, for this recipe.

Cut up and arrange on a plate:

> the green part of 2 green onions cut into
> 1/2 inch strips (the white section can
> go in the broth for flavoring)
> 1/2 of a boneless, skinless chicken breast
> into cut into 1/2 inch strips
> 1/2 of a large matsutake (Tricholoma
> magnivelare) cut into 1/2 inch chunks,
> remove the stems and the gills

In the fondue pot, combine and heat to a gently rolling boil:

> 1 small can, low sodium chicken broth
> 1-2 teaspoons soy sauce
> Add chopped up tops of the green onions

Prepare dipping sauce by mixing in a small dish:

> 1/4 cup soy sauce
> 1/2 teaspoon fresh ginger
> a small dab of wasabe or hot mustard

When the broth comes to a boil, thread a piece of chicken, matsutake, and green onion on a skewer and cook in hot liquid for 2 to 2 1/2 minutes or until chicken is cooked through.

Dip in sauce and eat.

Serves 2 or more

Gregg Ferguson's Stuffed Morels

A great recipe for a bonanza morel (Morchella sp.)year.

This stuffing could certainly be used to stuff other types of mushrooms such as portobellos (variety of Agaricus bisporus) or many other agaricus species.

3 pounds of 2 inch morels, cut into
halves lengthwise
3 ounces sweet butter
1 pound domestic mushrooms,
finely chopped
2 ounces sweet butter
1/4 cup white wine
1 pound pork sausage
2/3 cup bread crumbs
1/2 teaspoon dried dill
1/2 teaspoon dried oregano
1 pound cooked spinach,
drained and chopped
10 ounces Monterey Jack cheese, grated

Preheat oven to 400 degrees F.

Sauté the morel halves in 3 ounces of sweet butter for 10 minutes, trying not to break them. Remove from the pan and set aside.

In the same pan, add the remaining 2 ounces of butter, chopped mushrooms and wine and sauté the mushrooms 5 minutes, or until soft. Set aside.

Brown the sausage until all the pink is gone and the meat is well separated. Drain off the fat and add the chopped mushrooms. Simmer together 15 minutes.

Add the bread crumbs, dill and oregano, and toss well to blend. Add the spinach and cook 3 minutes longer. Remove from heat and let cool.

Stir in the cheese and stuff the morel halves making mounds of the stuffing mixture. Place on a cookie sheet and bake for 15 minutes or until the cheese is melted.

Serves 30 to 40

SOUPS AND SALADS

Soups

    Cream of Morel Soup   39
    Winter Mushroom and Chestnut Bisque   40
    Golden Matsutake   42
    Wild Mushroom Soup   43
    Mushroom-Coconut Milk Soup/Curry   44
    Bisque of Chanterelles   46
    Boletus Barley Soup   47
    Rumanian Tart Soup with Boletes   48

Salads

    Warm Endive Salad with Chanterelles,
        Enoki and Asparagus   50
    Boletos Caroenum, Hot or Cold Tree Fungus Salad   51
    Mushroom Tortellini Salad   52
    Lalap Djamur   54
    Grilled Corn, Asparagus, and Mushroom Salad   56

Cream of Morel Soup

1/2 cup onion, finely chopped
3 tablespoons sweet butter
1 cup fresh morels (Morchella, sp.), sliced
2 tablespoons flour
1 quart chicken stock
salt and pepper
1/2 cup heavy cream
6 tablespoons sherry

Sauté the onions in butter until clear but not browned. Add the morels and sauté for 6 minutes more. Remove the mushrooms with a slotted spoon and reserve.

Make a roux by adding 2 tablespoons of flour to the skillet and stirring vigorously with a wire whisk. Add the chicken stock, continuing to stir until thickened.

Add salt and pepper to taste.

Return the mushrooms to the soup and simmer for 15 minutes.

Just before serving, add the heavy cream and simmer until the cream has warmed. Do not overcook or the cream will curdle.

Add the sherry, stir 30 seconds and serve immediately.

Serves 4

Winter Mushroom and Chestnut Bisque

Contributed by Chef Joseph Cirone

1/4 pound shiitake (Lentinus edodes) or
honey mushrooms (Armillaria mellea),
sliced
1/4 pound hedgehog (Hydnum repandum)
or chanterelle (Cantharellus cibarius)
mushrooms, diced
8 large chestnuts, roasted
and pureed
3 tablespoons vegetable oil
1 large onion, diced
2 leeks, sliced
2 large shallots, minced
4 cloves garlic, minced
1 medium carrot, diced
2 celery stalks, diced
6 whole cloves
2 bay leaves
zest of 1 lemon
1 tablespoon black peppercorns
1/2 gallon heavy cream (you can
substitute whole milk if you must)
1/2 gallon chicken broth
2 cups blended scotch whiskey
2 tablespoons unsalted butter
1 teaspoon nutmeg
1/4 teaspoon allspice
1 teaspoon cinnamon
2 tablespoons white crème de menthe

Heat the 3 tablespoons of vegetable oil in a large stock pot and sauté onions, shallots, garlic, carrot, celery, cloves, bay leaves, lemon zest and black peppercorns, stirring frequently until browned.

Deglaze the pot with scotch and butter and reduce by 4/5. Add mushrooms and chestnuts and cook for 1 minute.

Add cream, broth, nutmeg, allspice and cinnamon to pot and bring to boil. Reduce heat to a simmer and cook for 30 minutes. Strain liquid through fine mesh strainer into a bowl and reserve the liquid. Remove the bay leaves, and puree vegetable matter in a food processor. Return liquid and pureed vegetables to the pot at medium heat. Season with salt and pepper to taste and add the crème de menthe.

Thicken with roux if necessary by heating equal portions, 1/2 cup of butter and 1/2 cup of flour in a saucepan and sauté until mixture no longer smells like flour. Whisk into soup.

Serve and enjoy.

Serves 12, but can easily be adjusted for less

Golden Matsutake

Contributed by Bob Sellers

Kombu, a type of seaweed, and Bragg's liquid amino can be found at most health food stores.

The vegetables strained from the soup could be served over rice.

To 1 gallon of water add the following chopped vegetables:

2 leeks (whites only)
4 to 6 stalks celery
1/2 pound carrots
1 small turnip
1 small parsnip
1/2 bunch parsley
kombu, 3-6 inch piece

Bring ingredients to a boil, reduce heat and simmer for 1 hour. Strain out the vegetables and reserve for other uses.

Add to the clear stock:

1/2 pound diced matsutake (Tricholoma magnivelare) (stems and caps)
1 heaping tablespoon of shredded fresh ginger

Return soup to a boil, adding water if more liquid is needed.

Before serving add:

Bragg's is a very salty substance, so add it to taste. If you can't find it, substitute soy or tamari sauce.

1 tablespoon tamari
1 tablespoon Bragg's liquid aminos
1 tablespoon sesame oil

Adjust seasonings to taste. Sprinkle with chrysanthemum petals and serve.

Serves 10 to 12

Wild Mushroom Soup

1/2 cup brandy
1 ounce dried morels (Morchella sp.), rinsed
1 ounce dried porcini (Boletus edulis),
   rinsed
5 tablespoons unsalted butter
1 1/2 cups minced onions
1/2 pound button mushrooms, thinly sliced
1/2 pound shiitake mushrooms,
   thinly sliced
2 1/2 cups (or more) rich chicken or
   duck stock
1/2 cup (or more) whipping cream
salt and freshly ground pepper
fresh lemon juice

Heat brandy in a heavy small saucepan. Add dried mushrooms and
let stand until softened, about 30 minutes. Drain, reserving liquid.
Rinse mushrooms and squeeze dry.

Strain soaking liquid through a sieve lined with a coffee filter, or
several layers of cheesecloth. Reserve.

Melt butter in heavy medium saucepan over medium-low heat. Add
onions and cook until translucent, stirring occasionally.

Add dried mushrooms, reserved soaking liquid and the stock.

Simmer gently 45 minutes to thicken the soup and blend the flavors. Puree the soup in a blender. Return purée to the saucepan
and add the cream.

Season with salt and pepper to taste and add the lemon juice.

Can be prepared up to 2 days ahead and refrigerated. Heat before
serving.

Serves 4

Mushroom-Coconut Milk Soup/Curry

Tom Yam Chieng Mai
Contributed by Chef Jozseph Schultz

This is a great dairyless alternative to creamed mushroom soup. It can be quite spicy, but needn't be. Adjust the chili and pepper to taste.

Galangal powder, a.k.a. zeodary, kentjur (optional). Available at oriental or Indonesian markets.

Except for the chanterelle (Cantharellus cibarius) and the bolete (Boletus edulis) the other mushrooms mentioned are now being commercially grown and can usually be found at many markets. The cremini (a form of *Agaricus bisporus*), shiitake (*Lentinus edodes*), oyster (*Pleurotus ostreatus*), and the enoki (a form of *Flammulina velutipes*) are readily available.

1/2 pound fresh mushrooms such as, cremini, shiitake, oyster, chanterelle, enoki, boletus. You can even substitute canned straw mushrooms, but why?
2 tablespoons peanut oil
3 cups thin coconut milk (recipe follows)
1 cup baby corn, preferably fresh, substitute canned or regular size fresh corn trimmed from the cob.
1 teaspoon garlic minced or paste.
1/4 teaspoon black pepper, freshly ground
2 leaves kaffir lime (available at oriental markets), or fresh lemon leaves or garnish with lime zest.
1 teaspoon salt, or to taste
1/4 teaspoon galangal powder,
1 cup thick coconut milk (recipe follows)
1/4 teaspoon roasted chili flakes, to taste (roast 1 tablespoon in oven at 350 degrees F. for 3-5 minutes.)
1-3 teaspoons fresh lime juice
2 tablespoons fresh cilantro or mint leaves
thick and thin coconut milk

Unfiltered Sake
(Tigers milk) would
be excellent with
this dish. Serve
Tigers milk chilled,
not warm. (You can
purchase unfiltered
sake in any
Japanese market.)

Shell a fresh coconut. Chop the meat.
Alternatively use 1 cup dry shredded
unsweetened coconut.

Place the dry or chopped coconut meat in
a blender with 2 cups very hot water, cover
and blend until smooth.

Strain mixture through a sieve into a
medium-sized bowl, pressing hard on the
pulp with a glass or bowl that fits the sieve. Reblend pulp with
1 cup cold water, strain mixture again and re-blend pulp with 1 cup
cold water. Strain mixture through sieve into large bowl, discard
pulp and let the coconut milk stand for 20-30 minutes. Skim off top
cup, this is thick coconut milk. Remainder is thin coconut milk.

Frozen coconut milk can be a good substitute, canned mediocre.

Wok mushrooms in oil over moderate heat until limp.
Add thin coconut milk, corn, garlic, black pepper, lime leaf, and
salt. Boil over high heat 5 minutes.

Add thick coconut milk, chili (taste as you go to adjust seasoning),
and lime juice.

Garnish with cilantro or mint and serve.

Serves 4 as a main dish, 6 as a first course

Bisque of Chanterelles

1 pound chanterelles
  (Cantharellus cibarius)
1 cube sweet butter (1/4 pound)
1 quart chicken stock
*4 cups *bechamel sauce*
1 tablespoon fresh parsley, finely chopped
1 cup heavy cream
1/2 cup sherry
salt
freshly ground nutmeg

Sauté sliced chanterelles in butter for 5 minutes. Transfer to a four quart saucepan. Using a slow flame, add the bechamel sauce and chicken stock, stirring gently to blend. Add the parsley. Cook just until all ingredients are blended.

Using a food processor or blender, blend the bisque so that all the chanterelles are thoroughly pureed and the color is a pale orange. Transfer back to the saucepan. Add the sherry and continue simmering for two to three minutes. Add the cream, cook on low heat for three minutes. Do not overcook the cream or it will curdle. Adjust seasonings.

Just before serving, sprinkle freshly ground nutmeg over each portion.

*Bechamel Sauce

In a medium saucepan make a roux of 4 tablespoons flour and 4 tablespoons melted butter. Slowly add 4 cups of hot milk, one cup at a time, stirring to thicken. Makes four cups of sauce.

Serves 4 to 6

Boletus Barley Soup

Contributed by Bob Sellers

1 1/2 quarts beef or chicken stock
1 quart water

2-3 large yellow onions, diced
1/2 head garlic (6-8 cloves), peeled and
chopped
1 cup pearl barley
2 teaspoons thyme
3/4 to 1 cup dried boletes (Boletus edulis)
1/2 head celery with tops, diced
3 small bay leaves
salt and pepper to taste

2 potatoes, boiled and mashed,
  for thickener

To water and stock add all remaining ingredients. Bring to boil for
15 minutes. Reduce to simmer for 45 minutes or until barley is soft.

Remove bay leaves before serving.

Serves 10 to 12

Rumanian Tart Soup with Boletes (Ciorba De Ciuperci)

Contributed by Chef Jozseph Schultz

This soup is great with a variety of mushrooms, such as chanterelles (*Cantharellus cibarius*), matsutake (*Tricholoma magnivelare*), the prince (*Agaricus augustus*), or hedgehog mushrooms (*Hydnum repandum*). If you use any of these types you may want to decrease or eliminate the boletes (*Boletus edulis*) altogether.

Jozseph Schultz

1 quart pork-veal stock (recipe follows.)
1 ounce dried boletus or other type wild mushrooms soaked in a cup of hot water for about 20 minutes, or 8 ounces of fresh diced wild mushrooms
1/4 pound assorted mushrooms sliced
2 tablespoons olive oil
1 large onion, diced
1 medium celeriac root, peeled and cubed sugar cube size (ask your produce man for celeriac root, he should be able to get it for you)
2 medium tomatoes peeled and seeded or 1 cup canned tomatoes
2 small carrots, diced
1/2 teaspoon dried thyme, or 1 teaspoon fresh, chopped
1 cup fresh fennel/anise stalk, diced
1/4 cup Italian parsley, finely chopped
1/2 cup sauerkraut juice plus ½ cup stock or 1 cup kvas (Slavic bread beer). Good luck on finding this one. I gave up and used the stock.
2 egg yolks, lightly beaten
sour cream for garnish (optional)
fresh dill for garnish (optional)

Sauté onion in olive oil with assorted mushrooms and boletus. Boil celeriac, tomatoes, carrots, fennel, thyme, onion, boletus in stock 10-15 minutes, until tender.

Add parsley and sauerkraut juice.

Garnish with sour cream and fresh dill if desired.

Stock:

The traditional stock for this dish is veal and pork simmered together for a couple of hours with carrot, onion, salt and pepper, a couple of bay leaves, and a tablespoon of marjoram. A pound or two of bones or a half-pound of meat per quart of water is about right. The best cuts for stock are bony, gristly, and cheap.

You can substitute chicken-pork, NOT beef-pork stock if you wish.

Vegetarians can substitute mushroom stocks; this soup is too good to miss.

Vegans add extra oil to soup, thicken it with cornstarch, and garnish with kosher sour cream.

Vegetarian Stock:

Cut up a mixture of some or all of the following: green pepper, onion, cabbage, carrots, potatoes, mushrooms (especially shiitake and shiitake stems) tomato, zucchini, celery. Wok the vegetables in a little oil until lightly brown. Add water, simmer and strain.
You can also make an easy stock from soybean (not mung) sprouts, found in oriental markets. Simmer with water and salt for about 5 minutes. Strain.

Soup serves 4 as a main dish or 6 as a first course

Warm Endive Salad with Chanterelles, Enoki and Asparagus

Contributed by Chef Joseph Cirone

One of the most unique salads in anyone's repertoire. The process for making the basil oil can be used to infuse the flavor of other herbs into olive oil. Once made it will keep for weeks.

Craterellus (*Craterellus cornucopioides*), with its earthy flavor, could also be used.

24 hours before serving

2 cups extra virgin olive oil
1 bunch fresh basil

Meat thermometer

In a saucepan over a low flame, heat the oil and herbs to 110 degrees (use the meat thermometer to determine temperature), steep overnight and then strain through a fine mesh strainer and reserve.

1/4 pound chanterelles (Cantharellus cibarius)
1 package enoki mushrooms (a variety of Flammulina velutipes which you can buy in almost any supermarket).
6 heads Belgian endive
1 bunch asparagus
salt and pepper
Parmesan cheese
baking soda

Blanch asparagus for 30 seconds in a large pot of boiling water seasoned with salt and 1 teaspoon of baking soda. Chill in ice water immediately.

Heat 2 tablespoons of reserved basil oil in a non-reactive sauté pan and cook chanterelles until soft and any moisture has evaporated. Season to taste with salt and pepper. Drizzle sautéed mushrooms over trimmed Belgian endive and asparagus that has been cut into 1 inch pieces. Garnish with enoki mushrooms and shaved Parmesan cheese.

Serves 4

Boletos Caroenum
Hot or Cold Tree Fungus Salad
Contributed by Chef Jozseph Schultz

"This recipe comes from ancient Rome. I can envision this salad being served to Nero at one of his many banquets by his favorite concubine. Ah decadence."

Jozseph Schultz

The concentrated wine gives an intense flavor to this salad.

1 pound mushrooms. Oysters (Pleurotus ostreatus) and shiitake (Lentinus edodes) are good in this dressing.
You might also try one of my favorites, bear's head (Hericium abietis).
1/2 cup caroenum (1 quart red wine, Chianti perhaps, concentrated down to 1/2 cup)
1/2 teaspoon black pepper to taste (it should be quite peppery)
3 tablespoons red wine vinegar or balsamic vinegar, to taste
4 tablespoons extra virgin olive oil
1/2 teaspoon salt, to taste
1/2 teaspoon fish sauce (optional)
a mixture of fresh baby greens, salad greens and spinach greens as a bed for each plate

Sauté all ingredients together over medium heat.

If sauce is too thin, strain out mushrooms and concentrate sauce over high heat until it reduces and thickens. Adjust flavor balance, add back in the mushrooms and serve warm or cold over the bed of greens.

Serves 4

Mushroom Tortellini Salad

Contributed by Shea Moss

For those of you who are not candy cap (*Lactarius fragilis*) fans, this recipe would work wonderfully with almost any other mushroom.

If you do not want to bother making pasta, wonton wrappers should work equally well.

1 pound candy caps
2 ounces sweet butter
2 cloves garlic, crushed
1 medium potato, boiled and mashed
3 tablespoons red onion, minced
6 ounces Parmesan cheese, freshly grated
salt and pepper

1 recipe *one-egg pasta, uncut

Dressing

1/4 teaspoon green peppercorns, roughly
    ground
6 ounces pepperoni
2 dried tomatoes
1/4 cup extra virgin olive oil
1/2 cup pine nuts, coarsely ground
3 tablespoons fresh, sweet basil leaves,
    finely chopped

Slice the candy caps and sauté in butter for 5 minutes. Add the garlic and saute 1 minute more. Remove from heat.

When the mushrooms are cool, put them in a food processor and using two quick bursts of speed, chop them into tiny bits.

In a large glass or wooden bowl, mix the mashed potato with the red onion. Then add the Parmesan cheese and sautéed mushrooms. Season to taste. Cool.

Cut the pasta into 2-inch by 2 1/2-inch rectangulalr wrappers. Make the tortellini by placing a scant half-teaspoon of the mushroom mixture in a wrapper and rolling up the rectangle into a tube. Form the tubes into little doughnuts by bringing the ends of the tube together, overlapping them by 1/2 inch and pinching firmly to seal. Let the tortellini rest for 20 minutes.

Gently slip the tortellini into a large pot of boiling water and cook until al dente. Drain them and put them in a bowl.

Slice the pepperoni, and place in a food processor or grinder with the dried tomatoes, and chop fine. Mix the peppercorns, olive oil, pine nuts and basil with the pepperoni, adding more olive oil if necessary to make a thick dressing. Pour the dressing over the tortellini and place in the refrigerator for several hours or overnight.

To serve, bring the tortellini to room temperature. Top with the rest of the Parmesan cheese and toss gently.

Serves 4

You can cut this recipe in half for the one egg pasta for making the tortellini, or smaller portions of any given dish.

*Pasta All'Uvo

2 cups all purpose flour
2 large eggs
3 to 6 tablespoons water
Additional all-purpose flour for kneading,
*   rolling, and cutting*

Mound flour on a work surface or in a large bowl and make a deep well in the center. Break the eggs into the well. With a fork, beat eggs lightly and stir in 2 tablespoons of the water. Using a circular motion, begin to draw flour from sides of well. Add 1 more tablespoon of water and continue mixing until flour is moistened. If necessary, add more water, a tablespoon at a time. When dough becomes stiff, use your hands to finish mixing. Pat dough into a ball and knead a few times to help flour absorb liquid. Then clean and lightly flour the work surface.

Knead dough by hand, 3 to 4 minutes, and sprinkle with flour if needed. Then proceed to pasta machine if you are using one. If you are using a rolling pin, sprinkle with flour and knead for 10 minutes or until dough is smooth and elastic. Cover and let dough rest for 20 minutes. Quarter the dough into balls and roll to desired thickness with rolling pin. Proceed with the recipe's instructions for cutting.

Lalap Djamur
Indonesian Mushroom-Tamarind Salad
Contributed by Chef Jozseph Schultz

Tamarind water is made by soaking 1/2 cup dried tamarind pods in 1 cup hot water for 10 minutes, then blending and straining through a sieve, or foodmill.

Tree ears (*Auricularia auricula*) can be purchased dried in Asian food stores, as can Galangal powder, also known as zeodary or kentjur.

1/2 head green cabbage, quartered and very finely sliced (optional)

3 tablespoons salt (optional)

1/2 pound mushrooms, whole if small or sliced if thick. Use cremini (a variety of Agaricus bisporus), oyster (Pleurotus ostreatus) or cep (Boletus edulis).

1/4 pound fresh tree ear (Auricularia auricula). You can substitute craterellus (Craterellus cornucopiodes) for the tree ear. Use 1 ounce dried, soaked, and stripped (optional).

2-3 tablespoons peanut oil

1 teaspoon soy sauce

1/2 teaspoon brown sugar

1/2 teaspoon garlic, minced

1 cup tamarind water,

1/2 teaspoon white pepper, freshly ground, to taste

1/2 teaspoon lesser galangal powder, optional

1-2 fresh green chilies, preferably jalapeno, finely chopped

1/2 pound cucumber, preferably English or Japanese, cut into thin rounds

2 tablespoons peanuts, roasted and grated

4 tablespoons green onions, fresh mint, or fresh basil finely sliced

Mix salt with cabbage thoroughly. Let stand 10 minutes, then rinse and drain completely, reserve and chill.

Wok whole mushrooms in peanut oil with salt or soy sauce slowly, or mushroom pieces a little faster, until juices render out and concentrate down.

Add brown sugar and garlic and wok briefly, until garlic starts to brown and sugar to stick.

Add tamarind water, white pepper, galangal, and optional chilies and wok over high heat until sauce thickens. Slightly over thicken; it will thin as it sits.

Let cool a little then serve on chilled cabbage surrounded with cucumber.

Serves 6 as a second course

Grilled Corn, Asparagus, and Mushroom Salad

1 ear corn, shucked
12 ounces asparagus, trimmed
8 ounces fresh shiitake (Lentinus edodes)
   mushrooms, stems removed
4 tablespoons extra virgin olive oil
4 cups shredded radicchio
1 tablespoon balsamic vinegar
1 small clove garlic, crushed through press
1 teaspoon grainy mustard
1/2 teaspoon coarse salt
pinch freshly ground pepper

When coals are hot, coat the corn, asparagus, and mushrooms with 2 tablespoons oil. Grill, turning as needed, until tender and browned (5 minutes for the mushrooms, up to 8 minutes for the asparagus and 8 to 10 minutes for the corn).

Cut the corn from cob and set aside. Cut asparagus diagonally into 1 1/2 inch lengths. Thinly slice mushrooms. Combine asparagus, mushrooms, and radicchio in a salad bowl.

Mix the remaining 2 tablespoons oil, the vinegar, garlic, mustard, salt, and pepper in small bowl. Drizzle the dressing over the salad and toss to coat. Sprinkle with the corn and serve at once.

Serves 4

THE MAIN COURSE

Fresh Swordfish Steak "a la Japonais"
        with Mushrooms   59
Braised Trout with Mushroom Sauce   60
Mushroom Stuffed Enchiladas   62
Crayfish Fettuccine   63
French-Canadian Meat and Mushroom Tart   64
Holiday Goose with Mushroom Stuffing
        and Grape Sauce   66
Oak Forest Pie   68
Eggs Benedict with Morels   69
Bacon 'N Bolete Quiche   70
Grilled Thai Seabass with Portobello Compote   72
Puffballs with Scallops and Broccoli   73
Glazed Chicken with Chanterelle-Sunflower Stuffing   74
Wild Mushroom Flan   76
Any Mushroom Pie   77
Sautéed Shiitake with Scallops   78
Chicken Baked with Chanterelles and Cream   79
Lasagna of Woodland Mushrooms over
        Balsamic Lentils   80
Squash-Mushroom Pie   83
Wild Mushroom Lasagna   84
Variations on a Theme—Basic Sauces with Mushrooms   86

Fresh Swordfish Steak "a la Japonais" with Mushrooms

Contributed by Chef Emile Mooser

You will need 4 8-ounce ramekins.

The combination of the shiitake (*Lentinus edodes*), the oyster (*Pleurotus ostreatus*), the enoki (*Flammulina velutipes*), and the honey mushrooms (*Armillaria mellea*) will not only be delicious to eat but will also be a visual treat with the blend of colors and shapes.

6 fresh swordfish steaks, 6 to 8 ounces each

Ingredients for marinade:

3/4 cup soy sauce
3/4 cup sherry
1 1/2 teaspoons grated ginger
flour for dredging

Ingredients for cooking:

1 large lemon
6 ounces sweet butter
6 ounces clarified butter
1 1/2 teaspoons grated ginger
1 teaspoon sesame oil
4 1/2 cups of mixed and sliced fresh raw mushrooms such as shiitake, oyster, enoki, honey mushrooms
chopped chives

Marinate the fish in the marinade for 15 minutes. Heat up the clarified butter in 2 large skillets. Flour each steak and sauté until done over medium high heat (don't overcook it), about 8 to 10 minutes. Place the fish on a plate.

In a separate pan melt the butter until lightly brown and foaming. Add the lemon juice, the mushrooms, ginger, sesame oil and sauté quickly. Add the chopped chives and spoon the mixture evenly over the fish steaks.

Serves 6

Braised Trout with Mushroom Sauce

Both the *Hydnum repandum* (hedgehog) and the *Craterellus cornucopioides* have lovely, distinct flavors which should blend well with the fish. Instead of the hedgehogs you might want to substitute *Boletus edulis* or *aereus*, or chanterelles (*Cantherellus cibarius*).

4-6 trout (3/4 pound each), boned
1 1/2 cups dry white wine
1 teaspoon Dijon mustard
4 ounces butter
6 shallots, finely chopped
1/2 pound craterellus, coarsely chopped
1 pound hedgehogs
1 leek, halved, and thinly sliced
3 tablespoons flat leaf parsley, chopped
Kosher salt
white pepper
1 teaspoon thyme
1 whole bay leaf
2 tablespoons butter
1 tablespoon flour

6 paper thin slices of lemon

Preheat oven to 450 degrees F.

Mix wine with mustard and set aside.

Melt butter in a pan which will be large enough to hold all the trout in one layer. Add shallots and leek, and sauté until soft but not browned. Add wine and continue cooking for 3 minutes. Sprinkle with thyme, parsley, salt and pepper. Remove from heat.

Sauté the hedgehogs in butter for 5 minutes on medium-low heat. Add the craterellus and continue cooking just until the mushrooms are well coated. Add the remaining tablespoon of parsley. Season to taste.

Put half the mushrooms in the pan with the vegetables and distribute them around to line the bottom of the pan. Fill the boned trout with spoonfuls of the remaining mushrooms. Lay the trout in the pan on top of the vegetables. Dot with butter. Tear the bay leaf into two parts, lengthwise, and lay on top of the trout. Cover the pan and place in oven for 20 minutes.

Remove the fish to a warm platter.

Make a roux of the butter and flour and add to the drippings, one teaspoon at a time, until thickened to the desired consistency. Pour over the fish.

Garnish with the lemon slices and springs of parsley. Serve with boiled new potatoes and crusty French bread.

Serves 4 to 6

Mushroom Stuffed Enchiladas

Contributed by Arturo Diosdado

For added spice use a small amount of seeded, chopped hot peppers. Do not use too much garlic as it will mask the mushroom flavor. Almost any mushroom would work with this recipe. However the shrimp Russula (*Russula xerampelina*) would be particularly tasty.

A vegetarian's delight!

Garnish with shredded Monterey Jack cheese, sliced radishes, sour cream and shredded lettuce.

How about a good Mexican beer to finish out the meal?

12 corn tortillas
soy sauce and salt to taste
1 tablespoon vegetable oil
8-12 ounces sliced mushrooms
1 medium diced onion
1 small diced green bell pepper
2 cloves chopped garlic
15 ounce can tomato sauce
15 ounce can of Las Palmas chili sauce

Sauté mushrooms, onion, and bell pepper in vegetable oil until translucent but not brown. Add garlic and cook another two minutes.

Add soy sauce and salt to taste, stir until blended and remove from stove.

Mix the tomato sauce with the Las Palmas chili sauce to taste (it's hot) in a small bowl. Dip corn tortillas in mixture and pan fry in a lightly oiled hot skillet on both sides until tortilla is soft.

Remove the tortilla and stuff it with the cooked vegetables.

Garnish and serve.

Serves 6 to 12

Crayfish Fettuccine

For those of you who don't eat Amanitas, some alternates might be the horse mushroom (*Agaricus arvensis*), *Russula cyanoxantha*, or even morels (*Morchella sp.*).

12 caps Amanita velosa, sliced
4 tablespoons sweet butter
2 tablespoons flour
2 cups seafood stock
1/4 pound fresh crayfish, shelled (tails only)
3 egg yolks
1 1/2 tablespoons freshly squeezed lemon juice
1/2 teaspoon pimiento, finely diced

Sauté mushrooms in 2 tablespoons butter for 7 minutes. Set aside and keep warm.

Using a 2-quart saucepan, with the heat on low, make the velouté sauce by whisking 2 tablespoons flour with 2 tablespoons melted butter. Add 1 1/2 cups fish stock, whisking to blend well. Allow the sauce to thicken, stirring occasionally. When the sauce is the consistency of heavy cream, remove from the heat and allow to cool slightly.

Purée the crayfish in the remaining 1/2 cup of stock.

Beat the egg yolks in a separate bowl. Then add 1/2 cup of the cooled velouté sauce and whisk vigorously. Do not allow the eggs to cook.

Whisk in another 1/2 cup of the velouté sauce. When it is fully incorporated pour the yolk sauce into the velouté saucepan. Add the puréed crayfish, lemon juice, and pimiento. Season to taste.

Whisking constantly, cook for 2 minutes over low heat. Then add the sautéed mushrooms and cook 4 minutes more, stirring often with a wooden spoon. Taste to correct seasoning. Pour over hot, fresh fettuccine.

French-Canadian Meat and Mushroom Tart

Suggested mushrooms for this tart are the prince (*Agaricus augustus*), blewit (*Clytocybe nuda*), or shaggy parasol (*Lepiota rhacodes*).

You will need a 9-inch tart pan with a removable bottom.

3 small new potatoes
1/2 pound lean ground pork
1/4 pound ground round
1 clove garlic, pressed
1 pound mushrooms, thinly sliced
1 cup red onion, coarsely chopped
1/4 teaspoon sage, chopped fine
1 teaspoon basil, finely chopped
1/4 teaspoon fresh rosemary leaves
1 teaspoon salt
1/2 teaspoon freshly ground black pepper
1 cup water
2 eggs
1 tablespoon water

2 9-inch pie dough rounds

Heat oven to 425 degrees F. Place rack in the center of the oven.

Coarsely chop the potatoes and boil them in salted water for 20 minutes or until tender. Drain, and whip with a whisk. Set aside.

Using a large heavy skillet, combine the pork, ground round, and garlic and sauté until browned. Drain off the excess fat and add the mushrooms and red onion. Cook another 2 minutes and add the seasonings. Stir well. Add 1 cup water, cover and simmer for 10 minutes.

Remove from heat and stir in the whipped potatoes and 1 egg.

Set aside to cool.

Press one of the pie dough rounds into the tart pan and trim the edges. Fill the dough with the meat and mushroom filling. Cover with the second piece of pie dough and trim and seal the edges.

Break the second egg into a small bowl and whisk with a fork until blended. Add 1 tablespoon of water and stir. Brush the top of the tart liberally with the egg mixture.

Bake the tart for 15 minutes at 425 degrees F. Then turn the oven to 350 degrees F. and bake for 30 minutes more.

Cool on elevated rack.

Remove tart from pan while slightly warm and place on a serving platter. Make a ring of sour pickles and watercress around the perimeter of the tart.

Serves 6

Holiday Goose with Mushroom Stuffing and Grape Sauce

If you use oysters (the mollusk not the mushroom) in your stuffing instead of sausage, use chanterelles (*Cantharellus cibarius*) and walnuts instead of boletes (*Boletus edulis*) and hazelnuts. Chanterelles give off a lot of water, use it in the reserved liquid.

6-10 pound goose
3-4 tablespoons garlic, minced
1 cup dried boletes soaked in 1 quart water
*   for 1 hour (reserve liquid)*
1 pound red onions, unpeeled
5 cups pita bread, shredded
1/4 cup fresh sage leaves, or 1 tablespoon
*   dried whole leaves*
6 tablespoons fresh parsley, minced
1 tablespoon salt
1 tablespoon freshly ground pepper
1/2 cup chopped hazelnuts
Optional: 2 sweet Italian sausages, cooked
*   to light gray and diced, or 8 ounces of*
*   fresh oysters, cut into pieces*

Preheat the oven to 350 degrees F. in order for water to steam.

Prick the goose all over with a fork. Place on a rack in a large kettle and add water to just below the rack. Do not allow the goose to touch the water.

Steam the goose for 1 to 1 1/2 hours. Watch the water level and add more water as needed. Do not allow the fat to scorch. Remove the goose from the pan and cool it on a rack.

Meanwhile roast the unpeeled onions in a 375-degree F. oven for 30 minutes. Cool, peel, and chop.

Turn the oven down to 325 degrees F.

Drain the mushrooms, reserving the liquid. Sauté the mushrooms and garlic in 1 tablespoon of the goose fat or olive oil, until garlic is soft but not browned.

Soak the bread crumbs in the reserved liquid, and then drain and press dry, reserving the liquid again.

Combine bread, onion, mushrooms, sage, parsley, sausage or oysters, nuts and pepper. Wet your palms slightly in the saved liquid and coat with salt. Rub the goose all over, inside and out. Stuff the goose and sew closed. Place in a roasting pan on a rack in the oven and cook slowly (about 15 minutes per pound), or until tender. Slow cooking is the key to a flavorful, moist goose.

Grape Sauce

reserved mushroom liquid
1/4 cup veal stock (or beef stock)
pan drippings from goose
2 tablespoons flour
1 cup red seedless grapes, crushed
1 tablespoon lime juice

Sauté crushed grapes in the pan drippings for approximately 5 minutes. Add the stock.

In a bowl, make a paste of the flour and 1/4 cup of the reserved liquid. When the paste is smooth add 1 more cup of the reserved liquid. Add this to the sauce pan and cook over medium heat, allowing the mixture to thicken.

Add the lime juice and serve with the goose.

Serves 4 to 8

Oak Forest Pie

Possible mushroom choices would include the oyster mushroom (*Pluerotus ostreatus*), chicken of the woods (*Laetiporus sulphureus*), and *Russula cyanoxantha*, a choice edible.

6 tablespoons hazelnut oil
3 cups mushrooms
  (one species or combined)
3 cups fine cornmeal
salt
3 whole eggs, separated
1/2 cup water
1/4 teaspoon garlic juice
2 tablespoons flat leaf parsley, finely chopped
1 tablespoon dill weed
2 tablespoons chives, finely chopped
1/2 cup sunflower seeds

Preheat oven to 375 degrees F. Position rack in lower half of oven.

Sauté the mushrooms in half of the oil until golden brown and tender. Season to taste.

Combine cornmeal, salt, egg yolks, and the rest of the oil with the water to form a soft dough. Press the dough against the bottom and sides of an oiled pie plate or small, square glass casserole.

Whip the egg whites and gently fold in the mushrooms. Add the garlic juice and herbs and season with salt to taste.

Fill the baking dish with the mushroom mixture. Sprinkle sunflower seeds over the top and bake for 40 minutes or until filling is firm.

Serves 4 to 6

Eggs Benedict with Morels
Contributed by Susanne Viverito

Morels (*Morchella sp.*) are a great complement to egg dishes. For a simple treat, sauté the morels and add to scrambled eggs.

1/4 cup fresh or reconstituted morels, sliced and sautéed in 1 tablespoon butter

Hollandaise Sauce

3 eggs, separated
2 tablespoons lemon juice
dash Cayenne pepper
1/2 cup butter

Separate the eggs and place the yolks, along with the lemon juice and cayenne in blender container. Cover and quickly turn the blender on and off. Heat 1/2 cup butter until melted and almost boiling. Turn blender on high speed and slowly pour in butter, blending until thick and fluffy, about 30 seconds. Keep warm over hot water until ready to serve.

4 eggs
1 tablespoon butter
2 English muffins
4 slices Canadian bacon
approximately 1 cup milk

Melt 1 to 2 teaspoons butter in a large, frying pan. Add milk to 1/2 inch. Bring milk to simmer. Crack 4 eggs into the simmering milk, keeping eggs whole and separate from each other. Simmer approximately 3 to 5 minutes until cooked to your preference, spooning some of the simmering milk over the eggs occasionally. Loosen the eggs from the bottom of the pan gently with a large spoon.

To Assemble:

Split the English muffins and butter them. Toast them under the broiler until they start to brown. Place 1 piece of Canadian bacon on top of each muffin and continue broiling until bacon is hot. Put 2 muffin halves on a plate. Place eggs on the bacon, and spoon the hollandaise over the muffins. Sprinkle the morels on top.

Serves 2

Bacon 'N Bolete Quiche

Contributed by Felicity Christensen

This is enough pastry for a lightly greased 8-inch quiche or flan pan with fluted edges and a removable base. This amount will also make 6 to 8 individual quiches.

Quiche Pastry

1/2 cup flour
pinch of salt
1 heaping tablespoon shortening
1 heaping tablespoon butter
cold water
beaten egg

Sift the dry ingredients together and rub in fat. Then add just enough water to bind and let it rest for 20 to 30 minutes in the refrigerator.

Preheat oven to 350 degrees F. and place a baking sheet on the rack in the center of the oven.

Roll out the pastry and line the tin with it, easing any overlapping pastry back into the sides if you can. Be careful to press firmly on the base and sides, then prick with a fork all over. Bake the pastry for 15 minutes, then remove it from the oven and paint the inside of it all over with beaten egg and put it back in the oven for 5 minutes.

Filling

This recipe is easily adaptable to what you have in your pantry. Once you have cooked the basics, you can add bits of anything you fancy—and boletes (*Boletus edulis*) are a great thing to fancy.

6-8 strips of bacon cooked dry and
*   crumbled*
1 heaping tablespoon butter
1 medium onion, finely chopped
1/2 pound of fresh boletes, chopped fine
*   (you can also use 3-4 ounces dry*
*   boletes, reconstituted)*
2 large eggs
10 ounces heavy cream
salt and freshly ground black pepper
freshly grated nutmeg (important that it be
*   fresh, if possible)*

Heat the butter in the saucepan and soften the onion in it for about 5 minutes.

Stir in the mushrooms and cook until all the liquid has evaporated (20 to 30 minutes). Stir frequently.

Combine bacon, onion, and mushrooms and transfer to the shell, spreading evenly.

Beat the eggs well and whisk in the cream. Season with salt, pepper, and a small grating of nutmeg.

Pour this mixture over the filling, put the quiche on the baking sheet and bake for 35 to 40 minutes or until the center is set and the filling is golden and puffy.

Serve straight from the oven if possible, though it does reheat quite well.

Serves 4

Note from Felicity: Most people fear the quiche because of the soggy-bottom syndrome. This can be eliminated forever by the simple expedient of prebaking the crust, always using a baking sheet underneath the tin and painting the inside of the crust with beaten egg and allowing it to rest for 5 minutes in the oven before the filling goes in. The container, whether you're making one large quiche or several smaller ones, should always be metal.

Grilled Thai Seabass with Portobello Compote

Contributed by Chef Michelle Dey

4 fillets Chilean seabass, approximately
   1 1/2 pounds
1 cup soy sauce
1 1/2 cups peanut oil
1/2 cup cilantro , chopped coarse
1 tablespoon sugar
1 teaspoon jalapeno, chopped fine
1 teaspoon fresh lemon juice
3 portobello mushrooms, sliced ¼ inch thick
1/2 cup green onions, sliced diagonally
1 tablespoon fresh ginger, minced very fine
1 tablespoon fresh garlic, minced very fine
salt and pepper
3 tablespoons olive oil for sauté

Start fire for grill

For marinade: Mix soy sauce, peanut oil, chopped cilantro, chopped jalapeno, sugar and lemon juice together. Marinate the seabass fillets for at least 1/2 hour to 24 hours.

Compote: Drizzle olive oil in a hot sauté pan and add ginger and garlic. Sauté for 1 minute, making sure not to brown the garlic. Add mushrooms, green onions, salt and pepper to taste and sauté until the mushrooms are golden brown and the onions are wilted. Taste and season with more salt and pepper if necessary.

When grill is very hot, add seabass fillets (reserve marinade) and grill on one side approximately 5 minutes (depending on size of fillets), flip fillets and pour marinade over grilled side making sure a nice crust of cilantro remains on the fish. Grill approximately 4 more minutes. Remove from grill and serve over mushroom compote with rice and fresh vegetables.

Serves 4

Puffballs with Scallops and Broccoli

Contributed by Shea Moss

The insides of the *Calvatia gigantea* (giant puffball) must be pure white in order to be safe to eat.

1 4 inch puffball
1 cup vegetable oil
pinch salt
bowl of water
1 pint chicken stock
1/4 cup white wine
3/4 pound scallops
2 tablespoons flour
2 tablespoons butter
1 teaspoon lemon juice
1 teaspoon sesame oil
2 heads broccoli, chopped
1 cup cream, or roux with 1 cup milk

Peel the puffball and cut into large chunks. Heat the vegetable oil to frying temperature (400 degrees F.). Soak chunks of puffballs, a handful at a time, briefly (about 15 seconds) in a bowl of water with a pinch of salt added. Fry until golden. Drain on paper towels.

In a 1-quart saucepan, mix the chicken stock and wine. Reduce the liquid to half of its volume by boiling rapidly. Remove and set aside.

In the same pan used for frying the puffballs, pour out all but one teaspoon of the oil. Stir fry the broccoli for about 2 minutes.

Dust the scallops with flour. Sauté them in butter and lemon juice. Add the stock and simmer for 3 minutes. Add the roux or cream and simmer to thicken. Add the puffballs and the broccoli. Cook one minute more just to make the ingredients evenly warm. Season to taste and serve over hot rice.

Serves 4

Glazed Chicken with Chanterelle-Sunflower Stuffing

If you use skinless chicken breasts, spray them with vegetable coating before putting them in the oven, and check periodically to make sure they are not drying out.

4 chicken breasts with skin

1/4 cup butter
3 tablespoons minced shallots (or onions)
1 garlic clove minced
3 medium chanterelles (Cantharellus cibarius), diced fine
1/2 stalk celery, diced
1/2 cup toasted sunflower seeds
1/2 teaspoon dried sage
1/4 teaspoon white pepper
2 cups cubed day-old bread

Preheat oven to 400 degrees F.

The stuffing is one of those easy to multiply recipes. You can also stuff a whole chicken or 2 game hens, or make it in a pan as a side dish.

Sauté the shallots, garlic, mushrooms, and celery in the butter in a medium pan until soft (about 5 minutes). Remove from heat and stir in the sunflower seeds and seasonings. Add the bread.

Place the stuffing mixture in a shallow glass dish or casserole large enough for the chicken breasts to lay flat over the stuffing and cover most of it.

Brush the breasts with a bit of butter or spray with vegetable spray. Bake for 15 minutes.

Meanwhile make the glaze.

In a small stainless steel or enameled pan, combine

> *1/4 cup sugar,*
> *1 tablespoon white wine vinegar,*
> *1/4 teaspoon cream of tartar.*

Cook over medium high heat, washing down any sugar crystals on the sides with a brush dipped in cold water. Cook until pale amber colored.

Remove from heat and add

> *3/4 cup fresh orange juice (one orange)*
> *zest of one orange*

Simmer for approximately 5 minutes on medium-low heat until orange zest is soft and glazed. Remove from heat and add

> *1/4 cup chutney*

Brush glaze over chicken breasts and continue cooking another 15 minutes or until done, basting with glaze every 5 minutes.

Serves 4

Wild Mushroom Flan

Contributed by Chef Joseph Cirone

You will need 4 8-ounce ramekins.

3 tablespoons clarified butter
1 clove garlic, peeled and finely diced
3 ounces shiitake (Lentinus edodes)
  mushroom caps, sliced
3 ounces portobello mushroom caps, sliced
3 ounces domestic mushroom caps, sliced
1 cup heavy cream
2 large eggs
1 egg yolk
salt, pepper
Italian parsley, chopped

Preheat oven to 400 degrees F.

Make a steam bath in the oven by placing a large pan filled with ½ inch of water in the oven.

In a large skillet, sauté the mushrooms, garlic and butter over moderate heat until cooked through. Remove from heat. Whisk heavy cream, eggs, and yolk together and add to skillet, stirring constantly. Season with salt and pepper to taste. Pour the mixture into ramekins and place in steam bath in the oven. Cook for 12 to 14 minutes or until browned and firm.

Garnish with chopped parsley and serve immediately, perhaps with a side of baby vegetables and a bottle of a fruity Chardonnay.

Serves 4

Any Mushroom Pie

The shrimp russula (*Russula xerampelina*) has a very distinctive flavor and would work very well in this recipe which is excellent for a vegetarian meal, accompanied by a salad. This is a very adaptable recipe. The flavor of any mushroom is sure to come out with this mild filling. You can also play around with different seasonings and herbs.

4 tablespoons butter or oil
1 large red onion, finely chopped
1 pound shrimp russula, coarsely chopped
1/4 cup all purpose flour
1/4 teaspoon salt
1/8 teaspoon pepper
1 teaspoon dried rosemary (or herb of choice)
1 cup light cream
1 cup chicken or vegetable broth
2 tablespoons white wine

1 9-inch pie crust

Preheat oven to 350 degrees F. and place the rack in the center of the oven.

In a large heavy skillet, heat the butter or oil. Sauté the onion until clear but not browned. Add the mushrooms and continue cooking until mushrooms are tender. Remove the mmixture to a bowl.

In the same frying pan, make a roux by sprinkling the flour in the drippings and beating vigorously with a whisk. Add the salt, pepper and rosemary.

Pour in the broth and continue whisking until the sauce is thickened. Add the cream, stirring constantly.

Add back the mixture and allow the mixture to bubble slightly to thicken. Add the wine, stir, and remove from heat.

Pour into an unbaked pie shell and bake for 30 minutes. Cool at least 10 minutes to allow filling to set. Serve warm.

Serves 4 to 6

Sautéed Shiitakes with Scallops

6 large shiitakes (Lentinus edodes)
    mushrooms, julienned
1 tablespoon shoyu sauce (can be found in
    oriental or specialty markets)
1 tablespoon cornstarch
1 tablespoon gin or sake
1/2 pound scallops
3 tablespoons light sesame oil
3 dried whole poblano chilies
    (your choice as to how hot you like it)
1 tablespoon fresh ginger, minced
2 cloves garlic, minced
1/2 red bell pepper, julienned
1 stalk broccoli, with stems and leaves,
    julienned
2 green onions, cut into fine strips,
    2 inches long

Combine shoyu sauce, cornstarch, and gin in a small bowl. Add scallops and let stand 5 minutes. Drain and discard shoyu mixture.

Heat a heavy skillet to medium high. Add sesame oil and red peppers and sauté for 30 seconds. Add ginger and garlic and continue cooking for 1 minute, or until garlic is golden.

Add broccoli. Sauté for 3 minutes, covered.

Add scallops and continue cooking, stirring gently for 2 minutes.

Add shiitakes and bell pepper. Cook for one minute and add green onions. Cook for 30 seconds and remove from heat.

Serve over rice.

Serves 6

Chicken Baked with Chanterelles and Cream

Contributed by Felicity Christensen

You might try some wild rice and asparagus as an accompaniment, along with a nice white wine.

2 tablespoons butter
1 pound sliced fresh chanterelles
   (Cantharellus cibarius)
2 tablespoons fresh lemon juice
2 tablespoons chopped shallots
   or green onions
1/4 cup dry vermouth
1/2 cup cream
1 chicken, cut into serving pieces
salt and pepper
parsley

Preheat oven to 350 degrees F.

Melt butter in a heavy skillet over low heat. Add the chanterelles, lemon juice and shallots. Cook about 20 minutes. Add cream and vermouth and cook another 5 minutes, mixing so that all the ingredients are well blended.

Place the chicken pieces in a shallow oven proof baking dish and pour the sauce over.

Bake 30 to 45 minutes basting occasionally.

Remove from oven and garnish with the chopped parsley. Serve immediately.

Serves 4

Lasagna of Woodland Mushrooms over Balsamic Lentils

Contributed by Chef Tony Baker

If you can't find the porcini mushroom flour anywhere, mix approximately 1 ounce of dried porcini powdered in the processor with 3 ounces of all purpose flour.

Pasta

14 ounces pasta flour or all-purpose flour.
4 ounces porcini (Boletus Edulis)
mushroom flour or substitute
5 ounces water
pinch salt and pepper
dash olive oil (I call a dash about
1/3 tablespoon)

Combine dry ingredients. Add water and oil. Knead until you have a nice dough. Let the dough rest in a bowl covered with a towel for one hour before rolling.

While the use of lentils is an unusual base for a lasagna, the mushrooms asked for, oysters (*Pleurotus ostreatus*), shiitake (*Lentinus edodes*), cremini (a variety of *Agaricus bisporus*) and porcini, the Italian for *Boletus edulis,* are wonderful to imagine together.

Mushrooms

8 ounces oyster mushrooms
8 ounces shiitake mushrooms
8 ounces cremini mushrooms
4 ounces porcini mushrooms (in season)
2 shallots chopped
1 tablespoon finely chopped garlic
1/2 cup Madeira
2 ounces tomatoes (concasse)
peeled and seeded
1/2 bunch cilantro
2 tablespoons butter

Sauté mushrooms, garlic and shallots in butter until soft. Deglaze pan with Madeira and add the chopped cilantro and tomato concasse. Continue to sauté for about 3 minutes.

Mornay Sauce

2 ounces butter
2 ounces flour
1 pint boiled milk
2 ounces Gruyere cheese, grated
1 egg yolk
Salt and pepper to taste.

Melt butter, add flour and stir to cook out the roux for about 5 minutes. Gradually add milk until a creamy consistency is attained. Finish by adding the grated cheese, salt and pepper. Add the egg yolk after removing the pan from the burner and blend. (Do not boil the sauce after the yolk has been added).

A good red wine is recommended with this dish. I think that the chef is entitled to sample the wine while putting all this together.

Balsamic Lentils

1 pound blanched green lentils
2 cups vegetable stock (you can buy
*   vegetable broth in most grocery stores)*
1 cup balsamic vinegar
1/2 cup carrots diced very small
1/2 cup shallots diced very small
1/2 cup celery diced very small
1/2 cup leeks diced very small
1/2 cup fennel diced very small
1 tomato peeled, seeded (concasse)
*   and diced*
1 teaspoon finely chopped garlic
1/2 teaspoon allspice
1/2 bunch cilantro chopped
1/3 cup olive oil

Sauté the carrots, shallots, celery, leeks, garlic and allspice in the olive oil. Add balsamic vinegar and reduce by two-thirds. Add the lentils, vegetable stock, cilantro, and tomatoes and simmer for 10 minutes.

To assemble:

You will need a soufflé bowl for each serving.

Roll out the dough into thin sheets (you will be making 4-inch discs with dough and will need 4 discs per soufflé dish).

Precook the sheets in boiling water, with a little olive oil and salt, until al dente, (about 7 minutes). Remove from water and immediately immerse in ice water to refresh.

Use a pastry cutter to cut the refreshed lasagna sheets into 4-inch rounds. Take the first disc and place it in the bottom of a soufflé dish, top with Mornay sauce, then a portion of the mushroom mixture, add another disc and repeat the process. Continue pattern. Finish the final disc by topping with Mornay sauce and grated Parmesan. Place lasagna under broiler until the cheese melts.

Turn the lasagna filled soufflé dish over a bed of the balsamic lentil mixture and spoon a little Mornay sauce over the top disc. Note that the layer with the Parmesan is closest to the lentils.

Serve hot with your favorite red wine.

Serves 6

Squash-Mushroom Pie

Summer squash, zucchini, or any similar soft squash will work. The mushrooms used should be very flavorful and could include *Agaricus subrutilescens*, *Agaricus bernardii*, and shaggy parasol *(Macrolepiota rhacodes)*. If you don't have enough wild mushrooms, fill in with store mushrooms *(Agaricus bisporus)*.

2 cups squash, thinly sliced
2 tablespoons olive oil
4 cups sliced mushrooms
2 cups cabbage, finely shredded
1 cup Gruyere cheese, shredded
2 large eggs, beaten
1 tablespoon fresh basil leaves, chopped
1/4 teaspoon rosemary leaves
salt and pepper
milk

2 9-inch pastry crusts for top and bottom. Place bottom crust in pie pan.

Preheat oven to 350 degrees F. and place the rack in the center of the oven.

Arrange the sliced squash in the pastry-lined pie pan.

In a large heavy skillet, sauté mushrooms, onion, and cabbage in olive oil for 5 minutes. Remove from heat and transfer to a large mixing bowl.

Add the cheese, eggs, basil, and rosemary. Season to taste. Mix well and pour over the squash.

Cover with remaining pastry and crimp edges to seal. Cut steam vents in top of crust, brush with a milk, and bake for 50 to 60 minutes until golden brown.

Cool on wire rack before serving.

Serves 6-8

Wild Mushroom Lasagna

Contributed by Bob Wynn

Many wild mushroom varieties work well for this dish. Suggested varieties would be boletes (*Boletus edulis*), chanterelles (*Cantharellus cibarius*), shaggy parasol (*Lepiota rhacodes*), or *Agaricus bernardii*. Portobellos (a variety of *Agaricus bisporus*) would also work.

Have ready

12 lasagna noodles, precooked in salted water
2 cups shredded mozzarella cheese
1/2 cup freshly grated Parmesan cheese

Bechamel Sauce

2 tablespoons olive oil
3 tablespoons flour
1 tablespoon chopped garlic
3 cups milk
1/2 teaspoon salt
1/4 teaspoon ground pepper
1 teaspoon Dijon mustard
1/4 teaspoon nutmeg

Heat the oil in a saucepan, add the garlic and sauté for 1 minute. Add the flour and cook the roux to a light brown. Add the salt, pepper, mustard, and nutmeg. Whisk in the milk slowly, 1/2 cup at a time, and continue cooking until the sauce is hot and smooth. Remove from heat. The sauce should not be very thick.

Mushroom Mix

1 tablespoon olive oil
2 cups chopped onion
1 tablespoon chopped garlic
1 cup chopped leeks
1 cup white wine
3 cups sliced mushrooms
1 teaspoon thyme
2 teaspoons fresh sage, finely minced
1/2 teaspoon salt
1/4 teaspoon freshly ground black pepper

Preheat the oven to 350 degrees F.

Heat the olive oil and add the chopped onion. Sauté until caramelized. Add the garlic, leeks, white wine and sauté another minute. Add the sliced mushrooms, thyme, sage, salt and pepper and continue cooking another 2 minutes. Remove from heat and taste for salt and pepper.

Oil a 9- x 12-inch baking dish.

Cover bottom with sauce and place first layer of noodles.

Coat with sauce, then spoon on some of the mushroom mix.

Add some shredded cheese and sprinkle with Parmesan.

Continue building layers, making certain to reserve enough sauce and cheese to generously cover the top layer.

Cover and bake for 45 minutes. Remove cover and continue baking another 15 minutes, or until top is browned.

Serves 8 to 10

Variations on a Theme— Basic Sauces with Mushrooms

Basic White Sauce—Good with Fish or Poultry

If lumps form while
cooking, whisk
sharply.

1 ounce butter
1 ounce flour
1/2 pint milk
salt and pepper

Heat butter gently, remove from the heat, then stir in the flour. Add the milk. Return to heat and cook gently for about 5 to 6 minutes. Bring to a boil and cook, stirring with a wooden spoon until smooth. Season with salt and pepper to taste.

Basic Brown Sauce—Good with Beef or Pork

Homemade beef
stock is best, rather
than canned.

1 ounce butter
1 ounce flour
1/2 pint clear brown stock
salt and pepper to taste

Melt the butter, add the flour, and stir into the butter and cook over low heat until golden brown. Do not overbrown or the sauce will have a burnt taste. The secrets are the low heat and the continuous stirring as the stock is added gradually. Bring to a boil, stirring constantly until smooth. Season to taste.

Adding the Mushrooms

To infuse the flavor of your favorite mushroom in the white sauce requires placing the stems of the mushrooms into the milk and warming on a low burner. Remove from heat and let stand covered for about 1 hour, adding additional milk to restore the full quantity. Strain and proceed with recipe instructions. For the brown sauce, infuse the stems into the stock. Another way is to add powdered, dry mushrooms (about 2 tablespoons) to the sauce while cooking, and then brown fresh mushrooms in butter and add right before serving.

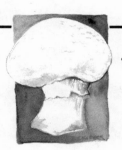

SIDE DISHES

Vegetables with Porcini Dressing   89
Fettuccine with Shiitake Mushrooms
        and Fresh Tomato Sauce   90
Yorkshire Pudding, San Francisco Dos Rios   92
Tagliatelle con Funghi   93
Mushroom Custards   94
Scalloped Potatoes with Sparassis   96

Vegetables with Porcini Dressing

Any vegetable, or a combination, would work well with this sauce. However, it would go particularly well with green beans or asparagus.

1/2 cup dried, chopped boletes (Boletus edulis) reconstituted in sherry, or 1 cup fresh chopped boletes

(After removing the boletes, the sherry could be strained and included in the sherry used to deglaze the pan.)

1 tablespoon butter per cup of boletes

1 teaspoon sweet basil (dried) per cup of boletes

5 finely sliced green onions

1 large clove garlic, mashed

1 cup sherry

salt and pepper to taste

1/4 to 1/2 cup virgin olive oil

Sauté the boletes in the butter in a medium skillet until thoroughly cooked.

Add the basil, green onion and garlic and cook 3 to 4 minutes or until the green onion starts to wilt. Remove to a bowl.

Deglaze pan with the sherry and return the mushroom mixture to the pan.

Gently steam your vegetable of choice until barely done and add to pan along with enough olive oil to coat the vegetables.

Stir gently until everything is heated through and serve.

Serves 4

Fettuccine with Shiitake Mushrooms and Fresh Tomato Sauce

Contributed by Chefs Julio Ramirez and Maria Perucca-Ramirez

Porcini (*Boletus edulis*) or oyster (*Pleurotus ostreatus*) mushrooms would make an interesting change in flavor and texture from the suggested shiitake (*Lentinus edodes*).

2 quarts water
2 teaspoons salt
1 1/2 pounds fresh fettuccine
4 tablespoons olive oil
2 tablespoons minced shallots
4 teaspoons minced garlic
3 cups shiitake mushrooms, sliced
2 cups fresh tomato sauce
1 cup diced tomatoes
1 teaspoon salt and 1/4 teaspoon pepper, or to taste
2 teaspoons minced parsley
4 rounded tablespoons freshly grated Parmesan cheese
1/2 cup Salsa Fresca (recipe follows)

Bring 2 quarts of water to a boil. Add the 2 teaspoons of salt, then the fettuccine. Stir, and bring back to a boil. Cook the pasta until it's al dente-about 3 1/2 to 4 minutes. (To check on the "doneness", cut one strand in half. The pasta is done when the center is cooked.) Remove the pasta from heat, drain and toss with 2 tablespoons of the oil. Reserve pasta.

Using two sauté pans, heat 1 tablespoon of oil in each. Add 1 tablespoon of shallots, 2 teaspoons of garlic, and 1 1/2 cups of shiitake mushrooms to each pan and cook until soft. Add half of the fresh tomato sauce, the pasta, the diced tomatoes, salt, pepper, parsley, and 1 tablespoon of the Parmesan cheese to each pan.

When the sauced pasta is hot remove from the heat and serve it on individual plates. Garnish with the remaining Parmesan cheese and 2 tablespoons Salsa Fresca per serving.

Serves 4

Salsa Fresca

Salsa Fresca is a flavorful, colorful salsa, which is used to garnish meat, egg and seafood dishes. It's also great as a dip for freshly made tortilla chips.

1 1/2 cups peeled and diced jicama
1 cup diced red onion
3 cups diced tomatoes
1/2 bunch fresh cilantro, chopped
3 serrano chilies minced
1/4 cup fresh-squeezed lemon juice
1 teaspoon salt
1/2 teaspoon pepper

Combine all the ingredients in a bowl, mix well, and chill. Makes approximately 6 cups.

Keeps for up to 5 days in the refrigerator.

Yorkshire Pudding, San Francisco Dos Rios

Contributed by Shea Moss

Boletes (*Boletus edulis*) or the aspen bolete (*Leccinum insigne*) would lend a hearty flavor to this recipe.

"This recipe was found written on the kitchen cabinet of a house I rented in San Francisco Dos Rios, Costa Rica.."
Shea Moss

1 cup your favorite mushroom, chopped
1 tablespoons butter

6 egg whites
6 tablespoons olive oil
1 teaspoon lemon juice
1 teaspoon salt
3/4 cup flour
1 tablespoon baking soda

Preheat oven to 350 degrees F. Place rack in center of oven.

Sauté the mushrooms in butter and keep them warm.

Whip the egg whites until frothy. Add the olive oil one tablespoon at a time in a stream until peaks form. Add the lemon juice and salt, and fold in the flour and baking soda.

Spoon into greased muffin tins and bake until golden brown.

When the puddings are done, turn out at once onto a serving plate, upside down.

Fill the pudding cavity with the warm mushrooms and serve immediately.

Makes 8 to 12 individual servings

Tagliatelle con Funghi
Ribbon Noodles with Forest Mushrooms

Contributed by Chef Clyde G. Griesbach

If chanterelles (*Cantharellus cibarius*) or morels (*Morchella sp.*) are not available, the flavor of the shiitake (*Lentinus edodes*) works quite well and makes this an international dish—Italian and Japanese.

3/4 pound butter
20 cloves garlic, peeled and crushed
2 pounds of forest mushrooms, sliced (chanterelles, morels or shiitakes work best)
2 tablespoons minced thyme
2 tablespoons minced Italian parsley
salt and pepper to taste
1/2 cup extra virgin olive oil, plus 1 tablespoon
Parmesan cheese for grating
1 pound Tagliatelle noodles

In a large pan, over medium high heat, heat the butter until foamy and sauté the garlic for 3 to 4 minutes . Add the mushrooms and cook for an additional 5 to 7 minutes.

Just before the mushrooms are done cooking, add the thyme, Italian parsley, salt and pepper. Set aside and keep hot.

In plenty of boiling water add the 1 tablespoon of olive oil, and a pinch of salt.

Add the noodles and cook at a rolling boil for about 4 to 6 minutes for "al dente," or follow the cooking directions on the package.

Drain and toss well, mixing in the 1/2 cup of olive oil as you toss. Add the sautéed mushroom mixture and continue to toss until well mixed into the noodles.

Top with freshly grated Parmesan cheese and serve hot.

Serves 4 to 6 as a main course, 8 to10 as a side dish

Mushroom Custards

Cantharellus infundibuliformis, known as the winter chanterelle, has the perfect delicate flavor for this recipe.

1 cup small, whole, fresh winter
   chanterelles (if the mushrooms are
   large, cut them in halves or quarters)
2 cups chicken broth
12 rock shrimp; or 8 small shrimp,
   cut lengthwise
1 tablespoon sherry
1 tablespoon soy sauce
4 large eggs
1/3 cup chopped celery root
1/3 cup finely shredded cilantro; reserve
   4 sprigs for decoration

You will need four ramekins or custard cups, and a bamboo steamer. If you don't have a steamer, create one by taking a large pot that has a tight lid and opening a metal vegetable steamer in it.

Bring the chicken broth to a boil and add the mushrooms. Reduce heat and simmer for 5 minutes. Remove and drain the mushrooms. Cool the broth and the mushrooms.

Plunge the shrimp into boiling water and cook them just until they become opaque. Remove them from the hot water and place them in a bowl of ice to stop the cooking. Drain them and divide the shrimp and the celery root into the 4 ramekins. Add two or three mushrooms.

Mix the sherry and the soy sauce into the broth. Stir to blend well. Beat the eggs until well blended and slowly add the broth mixture, stirring continuously. The liquid should not foam. If it does, let it settle for a bit before adding it to the ramekins.

Spoon the liquid into the ramekins to about 1/2 inch from the top to allow for expansion. Sprinkle with the chopped cilantro and cover each ramekin tightly with foil.

Place the cups in the steamer, cover and steam for about 20 minutes or until the custard is set.

Remove the foil and decorate each custard with one or two mushrooms and a sprig of cilantro.

Serves 4

Scalloped Potatoes with Sparassis

Contributed by Bob Sellers

6 potatoes pared and sliced 1/8 inch thick
1/2 pound cauliflower mushroom
  (Sparassis crispa)
2 cups shredded Gruyere cheese
2 cups heavy cream
1/2 cup chopped fresh parsley
1/4 teaspoon ground nutmeg
1/4 cup cup finely chopped scallions
2 cloves minced garlic
2 tablespoons cream sherry
1/2 teaspoon salt
1/2 teaspoon white pepper
1/4 cup butter or margarine

Preheat oven to 375 degrees F.

Alternately layer potatoes, mushrooms, and 1 1/2 cups cheese in lightly buttered 9 x 13 inch baking dish.

Combine cream, parsley, scallions, garlic, sherry, salt, pepper, nutmeg and pour over layered ingredients.

Sprinkle remaining 1/2 cup cheese on top and dot with butter.

Cover dish with aluminum foil and bake for 45 minutes.

Remove foil and bake 25 minutes longer until potatoes are tender.

Let stand 5 minutes before serving.

Serves 6 to 8

BAKED GOODS AND DESSERTS

Baked Goods

Candy Cap and Pecan Scones 99
Pine Spike and Potato Bread 100
Blewit Batter Bread 102

Desserts

Candy Cap Cheesecake 104
Candy Cap Cornmeal Loaf 106
Almond Candy Cap Cookies 107
Dessert Toppings 108

Candy Cap and Pecan Scones
Contributed by Shea Moss

1 1/2 cups fresh candy cap (Lactarius
   fragilis) mushrooms or 1/2 cup dried,
   reconstituted and drained
4 ounces sweet butter, very cold
1/4 cup brown sugar
1/2 cup chopped pecans
3 1/4 cups all purpose flour
4 teaspoons cream of tartar
2 teaspoons baking soda
1 teaspoon salt
1/2 cup milk

Preheat oven to 425 degrees F. Lightly flour baking sheet.

Slice candy caps and saute in 2 ounces of sweet butter until well
done. Add the brown sugar and continue cooking until the sugar
liquifies and bubbles. Remove from the heat and stir in the pecans.
Set aside and let the mixture cool.

In a large work bowl, sift together the flour, cream of tartar, baking
soda, and salt. Cut in the butter until the dough resembles coarse
meal. Add the mushrooms and pecans. Stir in just enough milk to
form a soft dough.

Turn the dough out onto a floured board and knead gently until the
dough is smooth and elastic. Roll the dough out to a thickness of
about 1/2 inch. Cut out scone shape or rounds using a 2 inch
cookie cutter.

Arrange the scones on the floured baking sheet, leaving space
between for the scones to rise. Bake for 10 minutes or until golden.

Makes a dozen

Pine Spike and Potato Bread

2 medium potatoes, scrubbed and diced
1/4 teaspoon salt
1 cup dried pine spikes (Chroogomphus vinicolor) and enough water to reconstitute
2 tablespoons active dry yeast
1/2 cup warm water
1 tablespoon molasses
3 whole eggs
1/3 cup vegetable oil
1 cup raw wheat germ
1 cup whole wheat flour
1 cup unbleached all-purpose flour
2 teaspoons salt
1 cup unbleached flour (a bit more may be necessary)
a small bit of milk

Cook the potatoes in boiling water with salt until tender. Drain potatoes in a collander, reserving the water.

In a small saucepan, cover the mushrooms with fresh water and simmer for 20 minutes until tender.

Put the potatoes and cooked mushrooms in the blender and purée thoroughly at high speed, adding a small amount of potato water, if needed, to ease blending. Cool mixture to lukewarm.

Prepare the yeast using molasses instead of sugar. In a large mixing bowl, combine yeast, eggs, oil, wheat germ, whole wheat flour, unbleached flour, salt and mushroom mixture. Beat vigorously with a wooden spoon.

Add enough flour to make a stiff elastic dough. Turn out onto a floured board and knead. Place dough in a well-greased bowl and turn to grease the top. Cover loosely, and let rise in a warm place until doubled in bulk.

Preheat oven to 375 degrees F.

Punch dough down and divide into six equal sections. Shape each part into a long roll. Place the ends of three of the together and pinch to fasten. Braid the three pieces together. Repeat with the three other pieces. Place on a baking sheet and let rise for 20 minutes.

Brush the loaves with milk and bake for 30 to 40 minutes, or until the bread sounds hollow when tapped. Cool on wire rack.

Makes 2 loaves

Blewit Batter Bread

2 tablespoons butter
2 tablespoons minced onion
1 cup cleaned and chopped blewits
  (Clitocybe nuda)
1/4 teaspoon dried rosemary leaves,
  crushed
salt and pepper to taste
1 cup evaporated milk
1 cup water
1/3 cup safflower or corn oil
12 ounces whole wheat flour
2 tablespoons dry yeast
1 1/2 teaspoons salt
18 ounces unbleached flour
untoasted wheat germ

Grease 2 1-quart casseroles or bread pans and sprinkle liberally with untoasted wheat germ and set aside.

In a heavy skillet sauté onions in butter until clear. Add the blewits and sauté until the mushrooms give off their water. Add the rosemary and season with salt and pepper to taste. Remove from flame and set aside to cool.

In a quart saucepan, heat the milk with the water, oil, and honey until warmed.

In a large mixing bowl, stir together the whole wheat flour, yeast, salt, and two tablespoons wheat germ. Beat in the warmed liquids with a wooden spoon. Add the mushroom mixture and continue beating to blend well. Then add enough unbleached flour until a somewhat stiff batter is formed. Pat the batter together with the wooden spoon, cover with waxed paper and let rise in a warm place for 60 minutes or until half again it's bulk.

Push the dough down with the wooden spoon and divide the dough into two parts. Slip each half into the prepared casseroles. Let rise again until the dough is even with the top of the casserole.

Preheat oven to 350 degrees F.

Bake for 35-45 minutes.

Run a knife along the sides and invert onto a wire rack. Let cool completely before slicing.

Makes 2 loaves

Candy Cap Cheesecake

Contributed by Debra Deis and Jeannine Bogard

This is similar in technique to making a thin marmalade. It is best to begin preparing the topping a day in advance of baking the cake.

Candied Candy Cap (*Lactarius fragilis*) Topping

4 cups (loosely packed) candy caps
2-3 cups sugar
1-1 1/2 cups water
1 1/3 cups coarsely chopped pecans
1 1/2 teaspoon vanilla

This recipe makes two 9-inch cheesecakes.

Clean and trim the mushrooms. Chop coarsely and place in a medium saucepan. Cover with 2 cups of sugar. Add only enough water to completely wet the sugar, about 3/4 cup.

Slowly bring to a gentle boil, stirring frequently, and cook 5 minutes. Turn off heat and let cool completely. Heat again to a boil and cook slowly until the mixture thickens a bit, 5 to 15 minutes. If mixture becomes too thick, add a little water.

This heating and cooling cycle should be repeated 4 to 5 times, adjusting the quantity and thickness of the syrup with additions of water and/or sugar. The final syrup should be the consistency of honey. Note: it becomes thicker as it cools.

Add the pecans at the beginning of the last cooking cycle.

Remove from heat and stir in the vanilla.

Any leftover candy cap mixture can be added to cookie batter or used as a topping for ice cream.

Preheat oven to 325 degrees F.

Crust

4 cups graham cracker crumbs
1/4 cup sugar
1/2 cup butter, melted

Butter the sides of two 9-inch springform pans half-way up. Sprinkle with a bit of graham cracker crumbs, shaking and turning the pans to coat the sides evenly.

Combine the rest of the crumbs with the sugar and the melted butter. Divide between the pans and pat evenly onto the bottoms. Bake 10 minutes.

Topping should be warm and the cake partially cooled at the time the topping is poured over the cheesecake.

Cheesecake

6 8 ounce packages cream cheese, at room
  temperature
1 1/2 cups sugar
3 eggs
1 cup sour cream
2 teaspoons vanilla

Beat cream cheese and sugar together until nearly smooth. Beat in eggs one at a time. Stir in the sour cream and vanilla. Mixture should look fluffy and smooth.

Divide the mixture between the prepared pans and bake at 325 degrees for 1/2 hour. Lower the heat to 300 degrees and bake until cakes puff slightly, 20 to 30 minutes more. they will be firm to the touch near the outer edges while the centers are still a bit soft. Let the cheesecakes cool slowly in the oven with the heat off. Or, you can hasten the cooling procedure by letting them cool about 10 minutes and then refrigerating.

When nearly cool, top with candy cap mixture. Resist making the candy cap layer too thick.

Candy Cap Cornmeal Cake

Contributed by Gloria Woodside

This makes a very strongly flavored loaf. For those of you who are not as fond of candy caps (lactarius fragilis), you might want to bake this delicious loaf without the mushrooms and make a sauce to serve with it (see pages 108-109).

Grind 1/4 cup dried candy caps until fine. Put them in a cup with enough water to barely cover and let sit 30 minutes.

2/3 cup soft butter
2 2/3 cup powdered sugar
  (sift before measuring)
2 large eggs

Sift together
1 1/4 cup flour
1/3 cup cornmeal

Preheat oven to 325 degrees F.

Generously grease and lightly flour a deerback pan or other 3 1/2 to 4 cup mold.

Beat butter until fluffy. Gradually beat in sifted powdered sugar.

Beat in the eggs and then the flour and cornmeal.

Stir in the soaked candy caps, draining off excess liquid.

Pour batter into pans and bake for 1 hour.

Cool 3 minutes and then turn out onto rack to cool.

Sift powdered sugar over the top.

Makes 1 loaf

Almond Candy Cap Cookies

Contributed by Barbara Hanson

11/4 cup crumpled, dried candy caps
(Lactarius fragilis) reconstituted in
brandy and drained, then sautéed in
1 tablespoon butter until dry
1 cup butter
2 cups light brown sugar
2 eggs, well beaten
3 cups flour
3 1/2 teaspoons baking powder
1/2 teaspoon salt
1 cup slivered, toasted almonds
1 teaspoon vanilla

Cream the butter with the sugar until light and fluffy. Add the eggs and beat until light again.

Sift the flour, baking powder and salt together and work thoroughly into the creamed mixture.

Stir in the candy caps, almonds, and vanilla.

Shape into rolls, 1 1/2 inches around, and wrap in plastic wrap. Chill overnight.

Preheat oven to 375 degrees F.

Slice the dough into thin slices and bake on greased cookie sheets for about 8 minutes.

Makes about 8 dozen cookies

Dessert Toppings

Vanilla Chanterelle Sauce
(Cantharellus cibarius)

An tablespoon of apricot brandy would be yummy added to this. If you don't want to use a liqueur, how about 2 or 3 chopped, dried apricots?

1 cup diced chanterelles
2 tablespoons butter
3 tablespoons honey
1/4 teaspoon vanilla

Gently sauté the chanterelles in butter for 10 minutes. Add the honey, stir just until blended and add the vanilla. Remove from heat and serve immediately

Candied Orange Craterellus Sauce
(Craterellus cornucopioides)

A dash of orange liqueur would intensify the flavor. Allow it to burn off. If the mushrooms are dried, reconstitute them in the liqueur.

1 1/2 - 2 cups chopped craterellus
3 tablespoons butter
zest from one small orange
1/2 cup sugar

Sauté the craterellus in 2 tablespoons butter until tender (5 to 10 minutes). Set aside.

Remove the zest from 1 small orange. Cover with cold water and cook until tender. Remove the zest from the water and drain. Make a syrup by combining 1/2 cup sugar with 1/4 cup water. Stir to dissolve. Add the zest and cook over low heat until the zest has a clear, candied appearance. Add back in the mushrooms and 1 tablespoon butter. Stir to blend ingredients. Add liqueur to taste. Cook another 2 minutes and serve.

Candy Cap Brandy Sauce
(Lactarius fragilis)

If mushrooms are dried, reconstitute them in enough brandy to cover. If they are fresh, add 1 tablespoon brandy while cooking.

1/4 cup dried or 1 cup fresh candy caps
   crumpled or chopped into small pieces
3 tablespoons butter
2 tablespoons honey
brandy, as needed

Sauté mushrooms about 10 minutes in butter. Add honey and cook until syrupy. Add the brandy and cook until brandy fumes are gone. Serve.

Serve over

vanilla ice cream
pound cake
cheese cake
or anything you'd like—use your imagination

Index to Mushrooms Used in the Recipes

The page numbers listed in parentheses indicate that the mushroom is an alternate suggestion for the recipe on that page.

Agaricus arvensis (63)

Agaricus augustus (48), (64)

Agaricus bernardii (83), (84)

Agaricus bisporus 26, 28, 76, (83)

Agaricus subrutilescens (83)

Amanita velosa 63

Armillaria mellea 0, 59

aspen bolete 92

Auricularia auricula 54

bear's head 51

blewit (64), 102

bolete 22, 30, 43 44, 47 48, 54, (60), 66, 70, 80, (84), 89, (90), (92)

Boletus aereus (60)

Boletus edulis 22, 30, 43 44, 47 48, 54, (60), 66, 70, 80, (84), 89, (90), (92)

Calvatia (Langermania) gigantea 73

candy cap 52, 99, 104, 106, 107, 109

Cantharellus cibarius 20, 31, 34, 40, 44, 46, 50, (60), (66), 74, 79, (84), (93),

cauliflower mushroom 96

cep 22, 30, 43 44, 47 48, 54, (60), 66, 70, 80, (84), 89, (90), (92)

chanterelle 20, 31, 34, 40, 44, 46, 50, (60), (66), 74, 79, (84), (93),

chicken of the woods 68

Chroogomphus vinicolor or C. rutilus 100

Clitocybe nuda (64), 102

craterellus   *24, 32, (50), 54, 60, 108*

Craterellus cornucopiodes 24, 32, (50), 54, 60, 108

cremini (var. of Agaricus bisporus)   44, 54, 80

domestic, store, button (cultivated)   26, 28, 76, (83)

enoki (cultivated)   44, 50, 59

horn of plenty   24, 32, (50), 54, 60, 108

Flammulina velutipes (cultivated variety) 44, 50, 59

giant puffball   73

hedgehog   40, (48), 60

Hericium abietis   51

honey mushroom   40, 59

horse mushroom   (63)

Hydnum repandum   40, (48), 60

the king   22, 30, 43 44, 47 48, 54, (60), 66, 70, 80, (84), 89, (90), (92)

Lactarius fragilis   52, 99, 104, 106, 107, 109

Laetiporus sulphureus   (68)

Leccinum insigne   (92)

Lentinus (Lentinula) edodes (cultivated)   17, 26, 28, 40, 44, 51, 56, 59, 76, 78, 80, 90, (93)

Macrolepiota rhacodes   (63), (64), (84)

matsutake   35, 42

Morchella elata, M. esculenta, and related species referred to as Morchella sp.   18, 36, 39, 43, (63), 69, (93)

morel   18, 36, 39, 43, (63), 69, (93)

oyster mushroom   28, 44, 51, 54, 59, (68), 80, (90)

pine spike   100

Pleurotus ostreatus   28, 44, 51, 54, 59, (68), 80, (90)

porcini   22, 30, 43 44, 47 48, 54, (60), 66, 70, 80, (84), 89, (90), (92) portobello (var. of *Agaricus bisporus*)   25, 26, 72, 76, (84)

the prince   (48), (64)

the queen   (60)

Russula cyanoxantha   *(63)*, *(68)*

Russula xerampelina   *62, 77*

shaggy parasol   (63), (64), (84)

shiitake (cultivated)   *17, 26, 28, 40, 44, 51, 56, 59, 76, 78, 80, 90, (93)*

Tricholoma magnivelare   *35, 42*

wine-colored agaricus   (83)

RECIPE INDEX

Almond Candy Cap Cookies 107

Any Mushroom Pie 77

Appetizers 15-36

Bacon 'N Bolete Quiche 70

Baked Goods and Desserts 97-109

Bisque of Chanterelles 46

Blewit Batter Bread 102

Boletos Caroenum, Hot or Cold Tree Fungus Salad 51

Boletus Barley Soup 47

Braised Trout with Mushroom Sauce 60

Budino Di Porcini e Tartufi 22

Breads
  Blewit Batter Bread 102
  Pine Spike and Potato Bread 100

Cakes
  Candy Cap Cheesecake 104
  Candy Cap Cornmeal Loaf 106

Candy Cap and Pecan Scones 99

Candy Cap Cheesecake 104

Candy Cap Cornmeal Loaf 106

Chanterelle Bacon 34

Chanterelle Caviar in Puff Pastry   31

Chanterelle Rice Paper Rolls   20

Chicken Baked with Chanterelles and Cream   79

Cookies
  Almond Candy Cap Cookies   107

Crab Stuffed Morels   18

Craterellus Paté   32

Craterellus Spread   24

Crayfish Fettuccine   63

Cream of Morel Soup   39

Custards
  Budino Di Porcini e Tartufi   22
  Mushroom Custards   94
  Wild Mushroom Flan   76

Dessert Toppings   108

Desserts   104-109

Egg Dishes
  Eggs Benedict with Morels   69

Eggs Benedict with Morels   69

Enchiladas
  Mushroom Stuffed Enchiladas   62

Fettuccine with Shiitake Mushrooms and Fresh
  Tomato Sauce   90

Finger Foods
Chanterelle Caviar in Puff Pastry 31
Chanterelle Rice Paper Rolls 20
Mushroom Strudel 28
Russian Blini 30
Smoked Shiitakes 17
Wild Mushroom Phyllo 19

Fish and Seafood
Braised Trout with Mushroom Sauce 60
Crayfish Fettuccine 63
Fresh Swordfish Steak "a la Japonais"
with Mushrooms 59
Grilled Thai Seabass with Portobello Compote 72
Puffballs with Scallops and Broccoli 73
Sautéed Shiitakes with Scallops 78

Fondue
Matsutake Fondue 35

French-Canadian Meat and Mushroom Tart 64

Fresh Swordfish Steak "a la Japonais"
with Mushrooms 59

Funghi Griglia con Polenta e Marscarpone 26

Glazed Chicken with Chanterelle-Sunflower Stuffing 74

Golden Matsutake 42

Gregg Ferguson's Stuffed Morels 36

Grilled Corn, Asparagus, and Mushroom Salad 56

Grilled Thai Seabass with Portobello Compote 72

Holiday Goose with Mushroom Stuffing
and Grape Sauce 66

Indonesian Influence
   Lalap Djamur 54
   Mushroom-Coconut Milk Soup/Curry 44

Italian influence
   Budino Di Porcini e Tartufi 22
   Crayfish Fettuccine 63
   Fettuccine with Shiitake Mushrooms and Fresh
     Tomato Sauce 90
   Funghi Griglia con Polenta e Marscarpone 26
   Lasagna of Woodland Mushrooms over
     Balsamic Lentils 80
   Tagliatelle con Funghi 93
   Wild Mushroom Lasagna 84

Lalap Djamur 54

Lasagna of Woodland Mushrooms over
   Balsamic Lentils 80

Main Courses 57-86

Matsutake Fondue 35

Meats
   French-Canadian Meat and Mushroom Tart 64

Mexican Influence
   Mushroom Stuffed Enchiladas 62

Mushroom-Coconut Milk Soup/Curry 44

Mushroom Custards 94

Mushroom Strudel 28

Mushroom Stuffed Enchiladas 62

Mushroom Tortellini Salad 52

Oak Forest Pie 68

Oriental Influence
  Chanterelle Rice Paper Rolls 20
  Grilled Thai Seabass with Portobello Compote 72
  Sautéed Shiitakes with Scallops 78

Pastas and Grains
  Crayfish Fettucine 63
  Funghi Griglia con Polenta e Marscarpone 26
  Lasagna of Woodland Mushrooms over
    Balsamic Lentils 80
  Wild Mushroom Lasagna 84
  Fettuccine with Shiitake Mushrooms and Fresh
    Tomato Sauce 90
  Tagliatelle con Funghi 93

Patés and Spreads
  Craterellus Paté 32
  Craterellus Spread 24

Pine Spike and Potato Bread 100

Portobello Mushrooms Mediterranean Style 25

Poultry
  Chicken Baked with Chanterelles and Cream 79
  Glazed Chicken with Chanterelle-Sunflower Stuffing 74
  Holiday Goose with Mushroom Stuffing and Grape
    Sauce 66

Puffballs with Scallops and Broccoli 73

Russian Blini 30

Rumanian Tart Soup with Boletes 48

Salads 50-56

Sauces and Topppings
  Variations on a Theme—Basic Sauces
    with Mushrooms 86
  Desert Toppings...108

Scalloped Potatoes with Sparassis   96
Sautéed Shiitake with Scallops   78

Scones
  Candy Cap and Pecan Scones   99

Side Dishes   87-96

Smoked Shiitakes   17

Soups   37-48

Squash-Mushroom Pie   83

Stuffed Mushrooms
  Crab Stuffed Morels   18
  Gregg Ferguson's Stuffed Morels   36

Stuffing
  Glazed Chicken with Chanterelle-Sunflower Stuffing   74
  Holiday Goose with Mushroom Stuffing and Grape
    Sauce   66

Tagliatelle con Funghi   93

Tarts
  Any Mushroom Pie   77
  Bacon 'N Bolete Quiche   70
  French-Canadian Meat and Mushroom Tart   64
  Oak Forest Pie   68
  Squash-Mushroom Pie   83

Variations on a Theme—Basic Sauces with
  Mushrooms   86

Vegetables
  Grilled Corn, Asparagus, and Mushroom Salad   56
  Scalloped Potatoes with Sparassis   96
  Squash-Mushroom Pie   83
  Vegetables with Porcini Dressing   89

Vegetables with Porcini Dressing   89

Warm Endive Salad with Chanterelles, Enoki
and Asparagus   50

Wild Mushroom Flan   76

Wild Mushroom Lasagna   84

Wild Mushroom Phyllo   19

Wild Mushroom Soup   43

Winter Mushroom and Chestnut Bisque   40

Yorkshire Pudding, San Francisco Dos Rios   92